WIDE AWAKE
IN SEATTLE

Success Stories of Outstanding Leaders
Who Learned to Share Leadership

WIDE AWAKE IN SEATTLE

Success Stories of Outstanding Leaders
Who Learned to Share Leadership

Kristine Sullivan Ed.D.
and
Johnna L. Howell

 **Integrity Publishing**
Seattle, Washington

WIDE AWAKE IN SEATTLE

Success Stories of Outstanding Leaders Who Learned to Share Leadership

By   KRISTINE SULLIVAN ED.D
AND
JOHNNA L. HOWELL

PUBLISHER'S CATALOGING-IN-PUBLICATION
(Prepared by Quality Books Inc.)

Sullivan, Kristine.
    Wide awake in Seattle: success stories of outstanding leaders who learned to share leadership / Kristine Sullivan and Johnna L. Howell.
    p. cm.
    ISBN: 1-886671-01-X

    1. Leadership. 2. Success in business—Seattle (Wash.) 3. Businessmen—Seattle (Wash.) 4. Women in business—Seattle (Wash.)
I. Howell, Johnna L. II. Title

HD57.7.S85 1996   303.3'4
                      QBI96-20446

LITERARY CRITIQUE: Judy Bodmer
COPY EDITING: Ann Koch
                           Weadonne Littrell

 Integrity Publishing
7456 E. Greenlake Drive N.
Seattle, WA 98115
(206) 524-5348 • (206) 524-5527 FAX

Dedicated to
Kristine's parents, Edward and Thelma Hansen
and
Johnna's parents, John and Weadonne Littrell
for their empowering love and support
over a lifetime

"In *Wide Awake In Seattle*, authors Kristine Sullivan, Ed.D. and Johnna L. Howell present the reader with an in-depth view of the soul of effective leadership. The authors invited leaders in both the profit and non-profit sectors of the greater Seattle area to tell their own stories of their journey to leadership. The genius of the book is that it is a rich collection of how personal value systems, philosophies and applied experiences shape the vision, mission and culture of the leader's organization. Thankfully, this is not a cookbook of so-called easy steps, but an intelligent reflection of various leaders' journeys to effective leadership. Each chapter will provide the reader with a solid evening's insight and learning."

—David Dunning, Ph.D.
Corporate Leadership Consultant

"An inspiring look into the lives of leaders who create success by freeing human talent. Gives me another reason to be proud of this city."

—Geoff Bellman
Author of *Getting Things Done When You Are Not In Charge* and *Your Signature Path*

"Your executive's stories convey the heartbeat of Seattle. They are inspiring secrets of effective mentors. They illuminate this civilized city."

—Bernard Haldane, Ph.D.
Founder, Dependable Strengths Institute.
Author, *Career Satisfaction and Success*

ACKNOWLEDGMENTS

Coauthoring this book has provided our own unique opportunity for collaboration. We were introduced by a colleague who knew that Johnna's professional experiences were in the areas of organization design, strategic planning, and high performance work teams. As a consultant, Kris had worked with leaders at all organizational levels to develop human resources and organizational goals. Her doctoral study, which featured in-depth interviews with outstanding empowering leaders, was mutually interesting.

During our first meeting we discussed how and why these men and women have gained respect for their achievements. We realized that we shared the belief that leaders can learn to influence the positive development of organizations and individuals who work together. We felt that the Seattle community had a story to tell.

The match was a good one, and the process has been deeply satisfying. We wish to acknowledge those who have enriched our understanding of empowering leadership as we produced this book.

LEADER IDENTIFICATION

These individuals are outstanding in their own contributions to the educational and business community. Their reflection and participation in this process account for the wide range of empowering leaders representing many Seattle organizations of varying size and function.

DR. CECIL H. BELL, Chairman, Department of Management and Organization, School of Business Administration, University of Washington

DR. PATRICK BETTIN, Director, Battelle Professional Development Center

VICTORIA COBOS, Partner, H.R. Services, Inc.

DR. FREDERICK DeKAY, Associate Dean, Seattle University Albers School of Business

DR. DAVID DUNNING, David Dunning & Company

DR. BEVERLY FORBES, Associate Professor, Seattle University Educational Leadership Program, Founder of Leadership Synthesis

DR. SARAH JOBS, Organizational Leadership Consultant

DR. KENNETH KNIGHT, Dean, School of Business and Economics, Seattle Pacific University

DR. ELIZABETH KONARSKI, Associate Dean, School of Professional Studies, Regis University, Denver. Formally honored by professional organizations in Washington state for success as an entrepreneur and business mentor

MARY ANN MOORMAN, President and CEO, Gamma Vision

J. SHAN MULLIN, J.D., Partner, Perkins Coie, Founding Member of Leadership Tomorrow

OUTSTANDING LEADERS

The leaders in this book have had the courage to *take a risk* and *take a stand*. Their insights as they have learned to collaborate in organizations add depth to the growing body of literature on democratic leadership. The stories are of interest to local, national, and international business leaders who are continuing to learn to develop others in accomplishing the productive work of organizations.

LEADER'S ASSISTANTS

Without exception outstanding leaders also have highly capable assistants. Their dedication to the philosophy of empowerment was demonstrated in concrete ways as they scheduled interviews, coordinated manuscript accuracy and approvals, and cooperated to meet accompanying deadlines. Their many anecdotes enthusiastically shared in the outer offices strengthened our understanding of daily collaboration in a supportive work environment. These capable individuals include NANCY ANTONELLI, CAROLYN DIBBLE, CLIFF DUGGAN, CAROLYN GOSSARD, ANN HOLMES, KATHY MARTINSON, MARK MURREY, PATRICIA PATTERSON, SUSAN PHILLIPS, MASS TAHARA, LOIS WHITE, and DIANE WILKINSON.

EDITORIAL CRITIQUE AND REVIEW

After the interviews were completed, another team of experts used the highest level of editing skills to preserve the integrity of the manuscript and the clarity of the information. Their expertise, supportive words, and humor at just the right moments helped to meet the goals of accurate reporting. Our heartfelt thanks to JUDY BODMER, CAROL HARBOLT, ANN KOCH, and WEADONNE LITTRELL.

OTHER WRITER/LEADERS

Intellectual debt is owed to business leaders and writers who continue to summarize what others have learned and who pose the next set of questions in the progression toward becoming a truly democratic community.

FRIENDS

Our appreciation to friends who have taught us over and over that vibrant communities are created by satisfying experiences in work, families, and friendships. We appreciate the interest so many have shown in this project. We are proud of your own leadership in a broad range of commitments, and value the renewal as we share the human side of our daily lives over a lifetime.

CLIENTS AND COLLEAGUES

As we learn to work together in a global community, we continually renew our skills, knowledge, and abilities through relationships with other professionals. These individuals teach us and challenge us as they model both technical and human aspects of leadership. Those specifically contributing to this project include Dr. ROBERT BARNES, Dr. JAMES CLARK, Dr. JOHN GARDINER, VERONIQUE GUILLAUDEAUX, Dr. BERNARD HALDANE, Dr. MILDRED HIGHT, Dr. GARY JUSELA, Dr. JOHN MORFORD, Dr. KATHERINE SCHLICK-NOE, JANIE SIZEMORE, BRONWYN SMITH, Dr. ROY WAHLE.

FAMILY

As we worked together, one of our heartwarming discoveries was that we both believed, as do many others, that many of the same empowering values that support successful businesses and schools are also part of satisfying family life. We have had the pleasure of participating in families which nurtured philosophical ideas and personal strengths in the mutual give and take of everyday life. The joy of life is truly in the journey and we deeply express our love and appreciation to our family members, who each have so much to contribute through their own unique talents and who support and care for one another in countless ways. Our source of energy for this project emerged from these continuing positive experiences.

Kristine's family include her parents, EDWARD and THELMA HANSEN, her mother-in-law, MARIE SULLIVAN, her husband, KEITH SULLIVAN, M.D., their children, LAURA, MELISSA, and PETER, and her sister, KAREN NELSON, and brother-in-law, WENDEL NELSON, PH.D.

Johnna's family include her parents, JOHN and WEADONNE LITTRELL, her mother- and father-in-law, MARVIN and BILLIE HOWELL, her husband, JERRY HOWELL, and children, JEFF and CHRISTINE, sisters, DONNA and DIANNA, and in-laws, CHERYL, RORY, MELISSA, and MARI.

CONTENTS

Virginia Anderson
Executive Director
Seattle Center

Reflects on experiences which led to her commitment to democratic leadership. Discusses the stages of implementing a strategic plan, with a workforce of over 250 full-time and 750 part-time employees, to develop the Seattle Center into a *preeminent event and destination place in the Northwest.*

Teresita Batayola
Former Director of Water Management and Planning
Seattle Water Department

Recounts early understanding of leadership principles when learning to supervise experienced employees with the Seattle Water Department. Continues to integrate elements of empowerment philosophy with nonprofit service organizations and City of Surabaya Water Supply Enterprises.

Phyllis Campbell
President and Chief Executive Officer
U.S. Bank of Washington

Discusses six core values which have become the foundation for creating an empowering work environment in a financial institution—banking. Gives examples of how employees demonstrating those values have been recognized and rewarded.

George Walker
Regional Vice President (Recently retired)
U.S. WEST Communications

Outlines career challenges in the telecommunications industry during "one of the most massive retraining jobs ever undertaken, before or since, in the history of the world." Defines leadership opportunities with a diverse workforce engaged in learning new technology, adjusting to merging company cultures, and mastering new work patterns.

Betty Woods
President and Chief Executive Officer
Blue Cross of Washington and Alaska

Describes the reality in competitive health care industry of simultaneously needing to lay off some members and empower other members of a traditional workforce. Outlines key leadership experiences in organizational change which emphasize empowering individuals with clear expectations for accountability.

INTRODUCTION

A smile comes to mind when thinking of the couple in the recent movie, "Sleepless in Seattle." The young man lives in Seattle and the young woman in Baltimore. They both lose sleep as they think about a potential introduction which might develop into a relationship that is more meaningful than the relationship each is currently pursuing. After many missed and awkward connections they do finally meet, and the moviegoer concludes the couple will be "sleepless" no more.

The stories contained in this book are not romantic like the one described above. Unlike the "sleepless" couple, the leaders in these stories are "wide awake." Their stories are authentic, real life successes. They have learned to make connections and share responsibilities in their organizations. They are respected not only by their stockholders, customers and communities but also by their co-workers. These leaders have demonstrated that achieving win-win working relationships is possible.

There are many reasons why Seattle provides fertile ground for studying leaders' productive efforts to collaborate. The young city, barely one hundred years old, is consistently rated at the top of "most livable city" surveys. With its mild climate, low crime rate, and scenic variety, Seattle draws vigorous individuals who are attracted to the beautiful lakes and mountains and the abundance of relatively inexpensive outdoor activities. During the rainy winter months, Seattleites turn to sports and culture; there are more art galleries, theaters, restaurants, and community music groups per capita in Seattle than any other city in America.

The appealing location draws top university graduates from all over the United States with the promise of challenging job opportunities and leadership development. There is an easy flow of ideas between high-tech employees in Seattle and those in the Silicon Valley. The Pacific Rim location provides relatively accessible cross-cultural learning amongst business leaders from various countries. These benchmarking cultural and economic exchanges between competitive economies encourage increased productivity, innovation, and creativity.

With some humor, local writers might suggest that Seattleites enjoy opportunities such as those available to Garrison Keillor's "wobegone" characters who are "all above average." The reality is that individuals in the Pacific Northwest face the same concerns as do those in other parts of the community and the world—learning to integrate developing technology and new work patterns in a global marketplace. In this relatively young west coast culture, a more democratic approach to leadership may be easier to implement because there are fewer layers of established competing power groups and stakeholders.

All of these factors have contributed to the rapid development of organizations committed to continuous learning. In an article on organizational change written over twenty-five years ago, Warren Bennis and Philip Slater predicted that a democratic organization potentially allows for the greatest range of ideas to flow continuously among diverse individuals in work groups. They felt this flow of new ideas would be especially important as pressures for collaboration continued to increase. In recent introductory remarks in *Leaders on Leadership*, Bennis emphasizes the point: "In the postbureaucratic world, the laurel will go to the leader who encourages healthy dissent and values those followers brave enough to say no. The successful leader will not have the loudest voice but the readiest ear. And his or her real genius may well lie not in their personal achievement but in unleashing other people's talent."

This book is a compilation of interviews with outstanding Northwest leaders who tell how they have learned to develop more democratic and empowering work environments. Most of the interviews were originally completed as part of Kristine Sullivan's doctoral study, *Empowerment AND Control: A New Management Paradigm,* which focused on the critical key experiences leading to these leaders' successes—experiences that eventually served to strengthen their belief in and commitment to empowerment. When interviews with additional leaders were included, the same interview questions were covered;

- the length of time the person had used empowerment strategies,
- the nature of their individual belief in developing others,
- what they did on a practical daily basis to increase productivity and improve services, and
- how they managed to sustain and renew themselves continually.

In the selection process, many outstanding leaders' names were submitted. Those selected represent a diverse cross section of leaders in key Seattle organizations varying in size, function, product, and services. Those nominated were respected men and women at the top of their fields. Names from outstanding leaders were obtained from "best company" surveys, academic experts, community leaders, employees, leading consultants and professional journals.

The interviews provide a valuable perspective on these leaders' thought processes as they learned to work productively with others. As the reader, you have the option to

- decide which specific aspects of the experience—technical or human—may be of interest,
- determine which ideas may be adapted to specific challenges in your own organization,
- evaluate methods and timing for transformation to a more democratic organization, and
- learn what does work and doesn't work for achieving democratic leadership.

With this perspective, then, you are invited to enjoy in-depth interviews with eleven of the most productive and considerate leaders in Seattle. These men and women have been "wide awake" to business and service opportunities in the local and international marketplace, and they are focused on the central question of the 90s: *How can we create democratic opportunities for developing organizations and people?* They are in demand because they lead organizations known for high levels of profitability and service. They are respected for working successfully through layoffs, restructuring, reengineering, retraining, and other organizational changes now common in diverse organizations. These outstanding leaders' personal accounts of their experiences include a wide range of refreshingly honest ideas which demonstrate they are, indeed, "WIDE AWAKE IN SEATTLE."

🐞 🐞 🐞

CHAPTER 1

VIRGINIA ANDERSON
EXECUTIVE DIRECTOR
SEATTLE CENTER
SEATTLE, WASHINGTON

Virginia Anderson grew up on the south side of Chicago as the eldest in a large family and attended public schools in her community. She completed an undergraduate degree at Southern Connecticut State College and a master's in Public Administration at the University of Washington.

Anderson began her career in the public sector, serving both King County and the City of Seattle in planning, budgeting, and project management. She moved on to the Cornerstone Columbia Development Company where she eventually became senior vice president.

As executive director of the Seattle Center, former home of the 1962 World's Fair and Space Needle, Anderson oversees the development and administration of Seattle Center activities. She began with a relatively stable staff of 270 full-time employees and over 750 part-time employees.

Anderson has been the catalyst for development of Seattle Center's master plan, the passage of a Seattle levy in 1991 providing redevelopment and construction dollars for major improvements to the campus, and most recently, the construction of the Key Arena, home of the Seattle Sonics. She has responsibility for an annual budget of $33 million.

Her volunteer work has been extensive, serving on such boards as Pacific Northwest Ballet, Seattle Housing Authority, Downtown Seattle Association, United Way of King County, and the University of Washington Foundation.

Anderson has received numerous awards and honors, most notably the Unsung Hero Award from the Corporate Council for the Arts in 1993. In March of this year she was named the Distinguished Alumnus by the University of Washington School of Public Affairs.

❦ ❦ ❦

You have quite an extensive background in both the private and public sectors. How has this background impacted your approach to empowering leadership?

One of the nice things about getting to this lofty age is that I can look back over my life and see the impact of my decisions—decisions that seemed inconsequential at the time. I can now see I have taken several significant turns in my life and career.

My first position following graduate school was with the City of Seattle Office of Management and Budget. The budget office was a new effort on behalf of the mayor. We were hired to create control over city departments that had not had central control and focus before and to create a sense of a united city strategy. At the time I was not aware of all the political implications of this effort. I only knew that I had been hired into an office that was very controversial.

I did that job through two budget cycles, and it taught me in very hard ways. I had to grow up fast professionally. I had to deal with some huge issues in one of "my departments"—issues that had major political implications. They were on the front page of the newspapers and we were vilified publicly in front of the City Council.

At one point the head of the department loudly and abusively berated me in front of his management group. Feeling that I was being unjustly and inappropriately attacked for simply doing my job, I realized that I had a choice to make. In the heat of the situation, I said, "You know, you are really upset right now, and when you calm down, I will come back, but I am not going to stay here while this goes on." I walked out. I went downstairs, and I was almost in tears. At the same time I was also completely calm. Since then I have often counseled individuals that there are alternatives to accepting angry situations. Participating only serves to escalate the anger. Individuals can absent themselves from the situation in a respectful way and choose to continue the conversation later when mutual goals can be accomplished. This experience taught me an important lesson.

A second lesson came in knowing I had done everything I could to right the situation. This was what enabled me to reach a place of calm even in the midst of anger.

The third lesson I learned was that this old-system, hard-edged organizational environment was also personally exhausting. I concluded that I did not want to work in this kind of organizational culture. I did not want to get used to this style, but most importantly, I did not want to become this style of professional. I decided that if this was what it meant to be a successful professional then I really did not care to be a successful professional. I learned a lot during this time. I mean, I *had* to learn a lot.

Once you had made the choice to change work environments, how did you decide what you wanted to do next?

I grew up in Chicago, and I mean *in Chicago*. We were from the south side which is a very poor neighborhood. Because of this I have always been an urban person and interested in urban issues. It was natural for me to decide to work on cities—on urban issues and city development. Eventually I was able to get a job working on downtown projects with Seattle's Department of Community Development. But I had had no previous experience in project management or development, so they took a real chance in hiring me. I got to work on some wonderful downtown projects and worked for two very strong, wonderful women, Karen Lane and Barbara Dingfield. Karen went on to become senior VP for development and community relations at the Fred Hutchinson Cancer Research Center. Barbara Dingfield is now manager of corporate contributions and community programs at Microsoft. It was fun to work for women who had different styles from each other and from myself. I have an enormous amount of respect for each of them and am grateful for all they taught me and for the joy of working with them.

During this time I worked on a lot of downtown projects and learned about community development. One of the key things that I learned was how to present visual images of potentially valuable civic projects to a diverse, voting public and to gain their support. I loved working with the business community, architects, and contractors. I loved putting things together and making things happen.

The job involved working with diverse groups of people, convincing them that this was a good project and getting them involved in the design process and funding. This process got everyone committed to making things happen. I liked the role of helping to create a visual image of something, getting people to see that image and be willing to pay for it, and then bringing that vision all the way through to reality.

Where did you go from there?

At that time the director of the department was Paul Schell and when he ran for mayor, I was one of his supporters for the mayoral race. After Schell lost that race, it was time to leave city government and I eventually accepted a position with his new private development company, Cornerstone. As Schell's first employee, I "grew with the company" and eventually became senior vice president responsible for oversight of marketing, development, and the property management staff.

Working on the rehabilitation of the downtown Tacoma area provided insight into the power of vision and leader-initiated communication. This critical experience marked a turn in my leadership development. In 1981 Paul and I went down to look at Tacoma and found it virtually dead. All the major retailers had moved out. There had not been any new building in a long time. There was no downtown hotel and the YMCA had just left. After analyzing this situation, we put together a project plan that ultimately became "my" project and as close to being "my child" as probably anything I will ever have. We had to pull it together quickly and propose the overall scheme for the Urban Development Action Grants (U-DAGs)—it was a *large* project.

The "Tacoma Center" project ultimately costing over $200 million included a hotel, a high-rise office building, a major rehabilitation of an old department store into office space, a new YMCA, and a public market. We also changed the streetscape, did two other rehab buildings, and later built the new headquarters building for the Frank Russell Company. Remember, I was fairly new at all this and was in charge of putting together this whole project and preparing our financing and grant applications. I had a team that had three architectural firms on it, three contractors, project managers, our leasing people, and city of Tacoma staff. We had an October deadline, so all summer we were doing a lot of work all at the same time. We put together the whole plan: did the environmental impact statement, completed the grant applications, got some costing information, and got a basic sense of where we were going so that we could begin to market the project.

How did the team respond to the tight timeframes?

Because of the pressure, team squabbles kept erupting. I was spending breakfasts with this architect, lunches with that architect, evenings with other groups—trying to keep everybody working and calmed down. All of the team members were basically having anxiety attacks.

How were you able to respond to their anxieties?

All of a sudden it hit me one night that *if* we succeeded—if we pulled this project off and made it work—everybody was going to feel good about it. If we did *not* succeed—if we couldn't make this project work, or get the needed funding or approvals—then no matter how many breakfasts, lunches, and dinners I spent with people—it wouldn't matter. The team would not have made it. It was an interesting feeling for me to suddenly recognize that the outcome of the project really depended on me.

So I went into the next meeting and said, "Okay. We've all got a lot of fears. We're all anxious. But this is where we are going. And when we get there, and when we finish this on this date, I'll be glad to sit with all of you and work through anxieties. But we're not going to do that now—right? Now, we are all going to do what we need to do to get us where we need to go. Right now I need each of you to do your part."

Maybe it was the opposite of what you would normally think about in terms of empowerment. All of a sudden I understood that they didn't need me to be their "friend." They needed me to *lead* them. They needed me to say, "This is where we're going!" and to show confidence. It was not okay for me to show them that I was scared to death and that I didn't know if we were going to make it work. That was not the role that they needed me to play. I needed to take care of my fears and concerns in a different way.

This sounds like a transitional time for you as a leader. What impact did these actions have on your relationships with team members?

It was lonely. My role with these people had suddenly changed. Many of them were architects I had worked with on other projects. They were my friends and we had been equals. Now, I couldn't be an equal with them in this process. I had to provide the sense of where we were going. I could acknowledge their disagreements and respect their opinions, but in the end I had to say, "This is where we're going."

Did this experience influence your view of team work and empowerment?

I have always believed that working as a team is the way to work when going through a design process. This is partly because I am a generalist. I don't have any specific skills. I'm not an engineer. I'm not an architect. I'm not a contractor. I'm not a computer person. I basically have very few skills, so I have to rely on others. I always bring together teams of people and then rely on them and their expertise. For example, I can remember a time when we were putting together a master utility plan for all these buildings. Even when I took physics in college, electricity just made no sense to me. My brain doesn't want to absorb it. So we were in this large meeting going through all the issues, and I turned to this man who was our electrical "whiz" and said, "Electricity makes no sense to me. I'm absolutely counting on you to get us through this one. You need to do this because I can't do it." He would have walked over burning coals. I mean, he was like the man on the white horse. He was going to make sure we were okay—and he did! I was aware that I needed to ask questions about the things I *had* to know. I also knew enough to know whom I could trust.

I also believed in the need for a design team meeting every single week. These meetings included the electrical, mechanical and structural engineers, the architect, and the contractor. I was told that it wasn't necessary to do this—that it was their job to coordinate with each other. I said, "I'm the boss, and we're going to have these weekly team meetings." The meetings worked because they maintained the work pace by answering questions and keeping everybody on the same track. Secondly, through these weekly meetings each contributor became an integral part of that project. They obtained a bigger picture of the overall project. We built all of the things we said would be built. Everybody was happy, and they had been part of a meaningful team.

As you grew as a leader of diverse professionals, were there other learnings that impacted your thinking?

When I was promoted to vice president I had what some call the "Cinderella Syndrome." I had a terrible fear attack. It was not about whether I could do the job. I had this blind confidence that with any job, you simply break it down into pieces and you can always figure it out. Now that I was going to manage more people, I was afraid I would lose myself as a woman.

This new position brought more responsibility as well as management of people who had previously been my peers. The challenge, or fear, was that—once again—I would have to separate myself from my peers and friends in a way that would allow me to be the boss. As the boss, I would have to say, "You did a *great* job!" or, "You *didn't* do a great job." At the time that I was dealing with the issue, my husband and I had to fly down to California and drive a car back. We talked about this issue most of the way back and that helped me to sort out my fear. I was afraid that I might lose the sense of myself as a caring, nurturing woman and that I was going to have to be very male and directive. Coming to terms with the fact that I could succeed with my style in this new role and that it would be all right was a very important step for me.

The second part of this learning was in making the transition from project manager to manager of project managers. I had been a great project manager because I kept control of every detail. For example, when we did the hotel in Tacoma, I was involved in property acquisition, testing the soils, submitting the U-DAG application, arranging the financing, picking the structural system, deciding how we were going to build the building, choosing all of the fabrics for the rooms and lounges, and handling whatever else came up. Now I was *managing* the project managers. I missed the fun of detailed involvement. To this day I love that part. I always want to pick out all those things and make those decisions. As a manager of others I could no longer do that if they were to succeed. I had to learn to trust people to take care of the details. I couldn't keep track of everything.

How did you transition to this new role of managing managers?

For a while I didn't know whether I would like this different role. It's important for people to ask themselves what they really like to do. I believe that you can't know how you feel about a new job for the first six to nine months. So I said to myself, "Okay, I'm going to try this job for nine months. *Then* I'll ask myself whether I like it or not and take the time to think things through." Once I got through the angst of giving up the details and trusting others, I decided that I liked management a lot. I like people management. Frankly, I like it on a big scale even more than I like it on a small scale because I want to do a lot of things. I want to get a lot of things done. I discovered that by managing *through people* I could get a lot of things done that I couldn't do singly.

What part did the goals of the organization play in your transition?

I have to believe that what I do is important. Money is not the thing that motivates me. I have to believe the project is important to a larger community. Cornerstone was a wonderful company to work for because we did wonderful projects. People used to scoff at us calling us a "private community development group" because we always did those "goody-two-shoe's" projects. We loved them, and we did a great job on them.

How were you able to later move from implementing ideas to creating your own vision? Were there certain understandings that you were able to embrace during this evolution?

At Cornerstone, as senior people for Paul Schell, our job was to sort through his many ideas and figure out which ones made sense and then make them happen. But we always counted on him to come up with the urban design vision and what the project should be. One day I asked myself, "Do I want to limit myself to implementing somebody else's vision or do I want to create and shape the vision? If I keep sitting back, I will never know whether I can do this myself or not." So I decided I would try making myself think about how I would do a project. I drove around town and when I'd see a piece of property, I would think, "Now, what would I do there?" I started making myself think in this way. In time I realized, "I can do this. I know how to do this." I also realized that, likewise, when you assume that you can't do a certain thing, then you can't. I then decided that I needed to challenge my previous assumptions.

How did this evolution impact your current work situation?

Emerging was not easy. It led to some pretty severe head bashing between Paul and myself. We had some challenges but we made it through every time. At first he was not accustomed to having people take on that realm of leadership in the company. In the end, I credit Schell with giving me the leeway to act on my ideas and to learn from my successes and failures.

Were you able to continue this professional evolution?

After nine years with Cornerstone, the company changed ownership, the real estate market changed, and I began to rethink my basic motivation. I realized I wanted to be involved in development projects that were about rebuilding. I needed to do something that met this need. It was at this time that I was hired for the position of executive director of the Seattle Center.

Now that you have taken on the responsibility for such a large workforce, how have you structured your management team?

I do something all of the textbooks on management say you shouldn't do. The books say you need management groups of eight and smaller, but our management team has talked about it several times and decided there are reasons for including all twenty-five people in management meetings. We know that this group is too big for true dialogue, but we can give out information and raise issues in that group size. It is a way of keeping people who are responsible for management issues informed about how those issues affect the whole. I have acknowledged to management team members that some of the information will be very boring to some departments, but it's important for people to know what is happening in somebody else's responsibility center. I've always relied on this open communication style—some would probably say, to a fault. It is something that I feel comfortable in doing, and it seems to work much more than it doesn't work: Therefore, I continue to do it.

Initially, what were your greatest challenges as executive director of the Seattle Center?

We originally set out on a very laborious process of developing a strategic plan. The plan literally came from the toes of the organization up. Everybody was involved. The first all-staff meetings were like firing squads. I remember standing up there and feeling like people were using machine guns to gun me down. I finally said to them one day, "You know, a lot of you have been here twenty-five years, and you're looking at me and thinking, 'Directors come, directors go. We're going to wait you out.' Your reasoning is sound. But, I *am* here now and while I'm here, we're going to work on these things."

What did you do to reinforce these statements and demonstrate your commitment to this new organization?

Slowly, through workshops and all-staff meetings, we eventually developed a mission statement, and then we developed major goals. We had 145 strategies on how we were going to accomplish our mission. One day we sat for eight hours working on our strategies. Forty-two people were there including crew managers, chiefs, and directors. We voted using a process in which each person had a buzzer. Every single strategy (145) was flashed on the board and compared against every other strategy. Each time we would vote on the most important strategy. We wouldn't move on to the next one until everybody had voted. It took forever and everybody's vote had the same weight as mine. The process was as important as the product. As our consultant said, we were trying to "get healthy." I'm not pretending that it came very quickly, because it didn't. It was a painful, long process. We've become a lot healthier and have come light years from where we were before.

The process you just described can be extremely time consuming. Do you continue to use this same process today?

We're now using a very different process as we re-work our vision statement. Our healthier state has allowed us to make a change. This time I have written the vision statement because we are using a leader-initiated, strategic planning process. I have also identified an issue of *management* versus *leadership* that needs to be addressed during this new process. We're doing a far better job of managing than we've ever done. My challenge is to support the progress they've made as managers and to move us to the next level by telling them that I now need them to be leaders. They have learned to *manage* a process. Now I need them to *lead* it. This is the next big challenge that we are facing.

What prompted this shift in your thinking?

Several years ago the City Council approved the Key Arena project, a $75 million project that spurred this shift to the leader-initiated strategic planning process. We had spent the previous fifteen months focusing on the project and obtaining final approval. Once approval had been obtained, there was a brief moment of jubilation—then I sobered up. Within about a week I said, "Oh my God. It's like the proverb: Be careful what you wish for—you might get it!" This is the first major public assembly building in the Northwest that will have to pay its own mortgage. The financing scheme we put together required that our annual budget, which was currently $21 million, would have to grow to $35 million in two year's time. We had huge challenges ahead of us.

I began thinking about the next two years. We needed to become a different organization. I called this our "transition period." I didn't know what that new organization would look like, but I knew that the existing one was not the organization it needed to be. The Arena was certainly the biggest single part of the challenge, but there was also a brand new children's theater and ballet facility, and we had just re-done the Northwest rooms and the entire courtyard. We had lived as the former World's Fair site for thirty-two years, and we needed to let everybody know that we were no longer the former World's Fair site. We were a very different place.

How did your staff make that transition?

I am touched by the staffs' openness to and enthusiasm for my taking the lead. I thought they might want the old process but things have changed. They tell me that I've now been here long enough and been "tried by fire." Most of the employees, including the electricians, painters, laborers, and overnight crews, now know that I understand their job issues. They listen to me and trust me. I've also recently emerged from a difficult situation with a renewed sense of confidence about my values and where I want to take the department. People are ready to let me take them there.

Where did you start?

Our previous mission statement included the phrase, "the professional operation of a premier urban park." The problem with that phrase was that we had to be more than "professional." We had to have a vision of what we are trying to be professional *about.* A premier urban park was not going to earn us $40 million a year. Our new vision statement says we are going to be *"the preeminent event and destination place in the Northwest."* This vision has come from the "top"—me.

Why is this change in wording so important?

The wonderful thing about the Seattle Center's mission is that it encompasses absolutely everybody. Our mission is to serve rich and poor, young and old, arts patrons, and sports fans. The very act of bringing all these people together as a community is one way we fight the "us/they" that is happening in the world today. It's a way for us to keep our sense of community, and it is unique to the Northwest.

What happened next?

After I completed the vision statement and made revisions following review and discussion with staff, our four division directors, in turn, created mission statements that described the mission of each of their divisions. These included statements of how that division's work enabled the department to achieve the overall vision. Their work, and the process of involvement and consensus building which was employed, created a leadership management "Aha" for me. I came to realize this was not about creating consensus. This was about leadership. If we had continued to develop the overall mission statement out of consensus, it would have ended up being the lowest common denominator of what we do. It would neither have been a "stretch" statement nor would it have been about things that we should be doing. We needed *leadership* now, not management.

I wanted them to think about this a little further. I wanted them to stretch. I asked them to think about what needed to be done within their divisions that might *not* be getting done now. I asked them, "If your present mission statement, with no title or indication of who it belonged to, was dropped on the campus and someone picked it up—could it be mistaken for a mission statement of an assembly line of Ford Motor Company or an IBM computer-producing section? Does it apply universally? Is it too generic?" I wanted them to be specific about the importance of what their division does as well as how they were going to do it.

What have you done to reinforce and support this request for more detailed mission statements?

We've been through this several times now, and they have had to go back to their teams and rethink and re-work their statements. Their managers are asking, "Why do we spend two hours on this if she's not going to approve it?" This has been an iterative process, and we're going to keep going at it. Some of the directors have invited me to come and talk with their teams about the vision and mission. I love to do this, but I need *them* to take on that kind of leadership role. They need to understand that I can't do this with everybody. I can't lead us all. I think that is the fallacy of many leadership books. They assume that one person can and should be the leader while others manage and follow. We need more leaders. I need the entire management team to *all* be leaders. Each one of them must own our vision. They've got to stop thinking, "This is what we've done and the way we have always done it" and start asking, "What *should* we be doing? What *can* we be doing in a new way?" *They* need to *lead* their people in creating the vision we want to have.

We're planning to take the entire management group for a retreat where we'll put together all of our transition work programs. One of the primary issues we're going to talk about is this need for broad leadership. I'm also going to change the name of the management committee to *leadership* committee. This may sound like a silly thing but I believe words do matter. I want them to see themselves as leaders and I want them to start thinking independently, just like I had to do with Paul Schell. I want them to have dreams about what we can be and I need them to own those dreams. They've got to want to make it happen, not just do what is required of them. It takes time.

You've talked a lot about the leadership group, tell us more about the involvement of the employees in identifying organizational values.

Our Employee Advisory Committee spent an entire year developing a statement of employee rights and responsibilities. It was important that they did this because if I or any of the managers had drafted it, the employees would have fought it tooth and nail. It is an incredible statement! It begins, "It's the right of every employee to be treated with respect and to demonstrate respect to everyone else." They emphasized both sides throughout the document. Every *right* is matched with a *responsibility*. They created a code of ethics as to how we will behave with each other. We're now trying to hold each other to that code of ethics. In fact, we have our first disciplinary case based on an employee's failure to live up to this new code of ethics. We are saying to one another, "This is the code we agreed to, and we're going to hold each other responsible for it." We're all equal partners in this venture.

It is *our* vision now. Every single person here now understands that whether they push a broom, process the invoices and pay the bills, or provide a stage setup for senior prom dances—they fit into the vision.

How has the organizational communication been handled during these years of change?

Over the years we've done a number of things to get more people involved and to share more information. We can never do enough. We implement new approaches. They work. Expectations are then raised and we just keep going. We started out with the basics—all-staff meetings. The meetings are voluntary, but we tend to get about 100-150 people at each. We've learned to be very careful about having a clear agenda, getting a lot of people involved in presentations and making the meetings fun, informative, and "safe." We've learned to do this in a way that is meaningful to staff.

We also put together the staff-elected Employee Advisory Council I mentioned earlier. The staff elect their representatives from different work groups all around the campus. They advise management on the whole spectrum of campus issues. They pick their own issues, elect their own chair, and speak for employees. There was also a lot of interest in doing fun things together during off-work hours, so we started a social organization called the Center Employees' Organization. They plan things like picnics, a Christmas party, dances, river-rafting, etc. In addition, we now have a cultural diversity task force that helps us think through how we deal with diversity issues and ways to celebrate that diversity. We also recently created an "employee development think tank." This is a cross-functional team focused on employee development and the question, "What can we do better as a department?" They recently came out with an elaborate report with sixty-five ideas. The challenge has been to determine how we'll follow up on all these ideas. When you create a means for staff to make suggestions and recommendations, you have to respond, even if to say "no," and explain why.

We also started an employee newsletter called *The Centerpost*. About three years ago, I started writing a column called "From the Director." Initially, I reported on things that had to do with the Seattle Center as well as some inspirational things. Two years ago I went to Africa and, when there, wrote my column from Africa. It was a very personal column about traveling in Africa, seeing all the animals, and describing what I loved about the environment. Everyone loved it. I got notes from people who thought it was great. It taught me to share more of myself.

I'm still amazed at how the employees respond when I let my passion go. They may not always agree with me, but they have a very keen sense about whether I am *real* about something. More than anything my currency comes from the fact that they know I will be *real* with them. If I disagree with them, I'll tell them straight and tell them why.

You have given us some examples of how employees have defined and managed rights and responsibilities. What happens when there is a need to handle really difficult employee problems?

Managers and employees now have guidelines for handling individual situations. As with many large organizations, there are always employees who are dealing with hopelessness, drugs, and/or alcohol, etc. In each situation we've been able to work with the union, the supervisor, and the employee. Together, we develop fair guidelines for employees to follow in their efforts to change habits and behaviors harmful to themselves or to the work situation.

We provide the resources, support, and understanding, but we also recognize that some people will not change. For example, there are a couple of managers that I've worked with now for three-and-a-half years, and I'm done—I am just done. They are civil service and they are union, so I've worked to find ways to deal effectively with their performance within the confines of those entities. I can't continue with them. It's not fair to the organization, and it's not fair to the employees they supervise. I keep saying to myself, "I owe it to the employees to create an environment where they are respected on the job." If a manager can't function properly, I'll provide the tools, the training, and the support. If he or she still does not change, then it's not fair to everybody else and I have no choice but to deal with the situation.

The hard thing for me is in recognizing that there are some people who simply can't succeed on the job. They're either so damaged from whatever may have happened in their past or have so much anger that they can't let go. There comes a point when you have to say, "This behavior is *not* okay. It is *not* going to work in this organization anymore." Where I fall down—and I'm known for this—is always trying one more time when others would have let go sooner.

As managers, we touch people's lives a lot. Forty hours is a lot of their week time to spend in one place. I may not be able to do anything about Bosnia, but I *can* do a lot about how employees are treated and respected here. We can give those who need some order in their lives a chance to feel good about where they work.

Work should be the one place an individual can have some order when other parts of their lives are failing. Sometimes I talk to individuals I know personally and give them examples from my own life. It feels awkward, but they need to know they are not alone. It helps immensely for them to talk to somebody. I have advised various managers they can help employees create a sense of control over their work even if their personal lives are in chaos.

How have your managers obtained the skills to handle these difficult situations?

We did first-line supervisory training for every supervisor to give them team management and conflict resolution skills. We also put five trainer/counselors on retainer to assist managers and supervisors in crisis intervention. When managers have a crisis, they only have to call me and I'll have someone out there immediately to help them resolve it. But I also tell the managers, "It isn't okay to let problems go until you have a full-scale explosion."

One of my long-term efforts is to continue staff development and to share a library of current articles and books on empowerment and related management issues. Books of common interest have provided a basis for a continuing dialogue among staff members at all levels of the organization. Overall, I feel that empowerment is not a simple concept or something quick that can be done to energize the workforce. I continue to believe that we are all part of a system. With care and thought, participation in an organization can evolve toward sustaining individuals as they work together toward the organizational vision.

Given the high level of energy needed to sustain the organizational vision, how have you sustained yourself on a personal level?

I understand hard work, so part of sustaining myself is about working hard. In addition, my grandmother, who was very religious, was very influential in my life. She taught me about spiritual things. I have attended formal church services at various times, but I'm not particularly involved in a religious institution now. I'm not a church-going type. I'm in a more spiritual plane now than I have been in a long time—not in a God-like sense but in an internal spirit sense. Poetry has also become more important to me. I also find that if I stay grounded in doing something I care about and understand why I'm doing it, then I'm okay. When I get too carried away climbing a career ladder and take the next "logical step" for career reasons only—then I get lost. I lose a sense of passion about my work. It's not that I can't do a good job in that situation. The job just isn't as sustaining when I'm not passionate about it.

What sustains me here is that I know what many of these employees' lives are like. My dad was a truck driver, my brother is a carpenter, and my mother supported us as a waitress for years. I'm passionate about being respected and respecting others. That is my passion for this job. People should feel they are fully human and not feel less than they are. When I get too far away from this thinking, I lose my passion.

Who do you look to for guidance in current organizational thinking?

I feel that Peter Senge's philosophy is accurate. Basically, he states: If empowerment is another efficiency tool, then it is another manipulative thing. It is *not* about valuing people as human beings, it is only about shaving off ten minutes. If we are going to have work environments which use people to do their best, it *has* to be because we care about them. We empower others because it is the right thing to do!

CHAPTER 2

TERESITA BATAYOLA
FORMER DIRECTOR
WATER MANAGEMENT AND PLANNING FOR SEATTLE WATER DEPARTMENT
SEATTLE, WASHINGTON

Teresita Batayola was born in the Philippines and educated in private schools until she was sixteen. Her parents immigrated to the United States, and Batayola applied to Seattle University as an undergraduate student. She was the first foreign student to be sponsored by the Seattle University Office of Minority Affairs. Staff members of that office advocated for her early acceptance to university-level work. She graduated *magna cum laude* from Seattle University with a B.A. in Public Affairs in 1973 and completed a master's degree in Urban Administration at Bucknell University in 1987. She also completed a National Urban Fellowship in Washington D.C., and has continued to participate in various management institutes. She is married and has a toddler, age 3, and a pre-schooler, age 2.

From 1973 to 1989, Batayola served in various leadership roles in government and community service organizations, including Tacoma Human Relations Commission, Bilingual Education Technical Assistance Center, U.S. Office of Personnel Management, Seattle Office of Intergovernmental Relations, National Pacific/ Asian Resource Center on Aging, Washington State Department of Licensing, Washington State Commission for Vocational Education, and Community Service Society of New York.

Batayola joined the Seattle Water Department in 1989 as senior executive assistant to the superintendent, and after holding a variety of managerial positions, she was named director of strategic services in January of 1993, and then director of water management and planning in June 1995. She was most recently responsible for directing the activity of the following divisions: policy and planning, conservation, water resources, and environmental management.

Since the interview Batayola has become a consultant with Montgomery Watson Inc. serving as the World Bank Strategic Development Adviser to the City of Surabaya Water Supply Enterprise, Surabaya Urban Development Project in Indonesia. Surabaya is the second largest city in Indonesia with a population of 3 million people. The Surabaya Water Enterprise is a semi autonomous municipal agency supplying piped water to about 40% of the population. Upon completion of the Surabaya Urban Development Project in 1999, the water system project will serve 92% of the city population.

Batayola has simultaneously participated in a variety of civic organizations that include the following: member, Governor's Citizen Cabinet and Washington Public Lands Advisory Committee; executive committee member, Western Urban Water Coalition; 1993 conference chair, American Water Works Association, Pacific Northwest Section; and past chair, the International District

Preservation Development Authority. Her past service includes the Northwest Women's Law Center, Asian Counseling and Referral Service, the State Centennial Commission Public Relations Committee, and numerous other boards and task forces.

Batayola has received numerous awards for her contributions, including *International Examiner* Volunteer of the Year (1985); Service Recognition, International District Preservation Development Authority (1993); named 1994 VIP (Very Important Pinoy) by the Filipino American National Historic Association; and nominated for the 1995 Seattle Management Association's Outstanding Award for management leadership and innovation.

How have you been able to relate the concept of empowerment to your work experiences?

I perceive myself to be a high-control person and rather than trying to control people, I try to control assignments, expectations, environment, schedule timelines, deadlines, and quality of product. There are also times when I need to be controlling with people, but there are times when I allow people to fail and it becomes a mutual learning experience.

Some examples of my early experiences in empowering others include my involvement in the community as a volunteer and as a supervisor of volunteers. From the very beginning I needed to learn a lot of patience when allowing people to do things their own way. The bottom line was I had to accept that there were all sorts of ways to do things, not just the way I envisioned doing them. That was hard for me to learn because I tend to be energetic and to want things done right now. I learned to give up my view of perfection and to adjust my expectations. When you work with volunteers, you don't have many "carrots" for them, so I had to learn to negotiate with the volunteers to get to a mutually satisfactory goal.

In terms of work experience, the very first time I had an official supervisory title was at the age of twenty-eight. I was public affairs administrator for the State Department of Licensing. In this position I supervised employees who were civil service, and I soon recognized the need to cultivate relationships. Two of the women who reported to me made a dramatic impact on my learning about supervision and empowerment.

One of my staff, the most senior one, was a woman who was approximately ten years older than I. She had previously been the administrator but lost the job when a new state governor took over. She still had a job but it no longer carried the title of administrator. The other woman was a long-term employee who had been with the state fourteen years and had worked into a paraprofessional position. The first time we got together she told me that she didn't like change.

Both of these women had strong personalities. With the senior person, I decided not to "manage her" as she was already very well established. What I tried to do, instead, was to cultivate a more collegial relationship. I knew I would have to be very diplomatic, so any time there were official functions, I chose to take her with me. I treated her more like a partner. At the time I was running on instinct because I was too young to really know what I was doing. In the meantime, I was also learning quite a bit as I was doing it.

This is fresh in my mind because when someone called me for a reference on this person, I realized that had I not culti- vated a collegial relationship, I would not have fared as well in that position.

I approached the one who didn't like change differently. First of all, I didn't like the fact that she had laid down the gauntlet early on. Because of this, I chose to take a much more traditional supervisory route. I initially asked her to tell me about her job and to explain why she does what she does. I also talked to her about my expectations. I found out later that she had initially been moved into her position because she had whined enough. Sometimes this actually works. The per- son is promoted, and the supervisor says, "See, I've done some- thing for you—now enough!"

But I also wanted to give her a chance, so I sent her to training classes to improve her skills. I also provided ongoing feedback regarding her performance and her need for improve- ment. In spite of this support I ended up giving her a mediocre first performance evaluation. I believe it is possible to counsel and talk with people about their performance, but often, they don't really hear unless they see it on paper. This may seem like a broad generalization, but in government there are so many people who work just enough to get by. In fact, she told me exactly how many years she needed to work before she could retire. When she was faced with a mediocre performance review, her sense of security was threatened.

As you look back over these decisions, would you have done anything differently?

In the first instance, I would not have done anything differently. She was very competent and continues to be successful. We have continued to have a good relationship. In the other situation I probably would have transferred her. If I could have predicted how much time and energy it would take to coach, cajole, persuade, and threaten, I would not have continued. At that time I had an unrealistic expectation. I believed that, given the right amount of support and tools for the job, you could bring a person up to a certain performance level. Now I realize that as a manager, you really do need to look at a person's potential and capabilities, and determine how far you can reasonably support the employee. In the second case, I would still start off the same way and give the person the opportunity to show she could do something, and I would provide what she needed, whether that was training or having more challenges or better equipment. But I would also want to see actual results.

Where did you go from there?

Again, there was a change in government and a new governor. As an appointee of the previous governor, I lost my job. Because of my professional network, however, I was immediately offered another position. This was in economic development for the Commission for Vocational Education. The new governor's emphasis was on economic development. We worked on projects with small businesses, agriculture, and the timber industry and I traveled the state constantly. This was during the recession, and I was only occasionally in Seattle. In that particular job I had to work constantly with businesses and with local community colleges to develop programs which would help an area turn around economically. My particular focus was economic development, particularly small business incubators and retraining programs.

Then I burned out. In one year alone I traveled over 50,000 miles in Washington. In addition, the kinds of jobs I'd held had not been conducive to developing personal relationships. I had gained some measure of prominence in Seattle because of my community involvements, but I was also feeling a lot of stress in terms of expectations. So to get a bearing on myself, I decided to go to New York.

Coincidentally, it was also the seventh year of my master's program and if I didn't finish my thesis within the year, I would lose the opportunity to complete my degree. Because my graduate work was with Bucknell University in Pennsylvania, I had a double reason to move to the east coast.

While completing my degree at Bucknell, I also worked as director of public relations for a non-profit community services agency in New York that was 140 years old. It was a very well-endowed agency with a budget of over $12 million. In the beginning it had mainly served the needs of European immigrants. When I started, it was undergoing an identity crisis and a mission change. In an unexpected way I learned a lot about understanding the needs of other minority groups in a highly polarized city. A lot of the supporters represented old-line money in the community, but the people they served had changed drastically. They were now African Americans, Asian Americans, and Latin Americans. We had many new staff members, and we brought in new blood, including a new director who was a Harvard-trained African American lawyer. They were taking some major steps toward transformation.

The empowerment issues that we dealt with there were not only in the context of joblessness and homelessness but also with the long-term "dis-education" of children. We're talking here about a generation of kids who, even if they had made it to school, were not getting a good education. We worked with a system of school community boards in which one didn't have to be a citizen to participate. If you were a parent you could be involved. But the parents we worked with were poor and had little education, so it was a huge job to get them to understand that they could get involved. It was very educational for me to work in a situation where the gaps between cultures were so huge.

How is it that you ended up back in Seattle?

I came back to Seattle to be with my husband to-be. It was really a value-based decision and a life style decision.

You have certainly had some wonderful experiences and opportunities. Tell us about your current position. How were you able to progress so quickly in this organization?

When I started with the Seattle Water Department six years ago, I was hired as the senior executive assistant to the superintendent. When I got that job, I knew that it would be a dream for me because as the superintendent's right arm, I could do all kinds of things in the organization and it turned out exactly that way because he was empowering. Any project I wanted to do, I would pitch it and, if it was reasonable, get agreement. Because of my willingness to step forward with ideas and plans, he started to accelerate my responsibilities. During this time he initiated the formation of a public information group. I had the responsibility for its centralization and eventually became the division director overseeing community relations as well as human resources, conservation, and policy and planning.

At the beginning of that same year, a new superintendent, appointed by the mayor, took office. She reorganized the department and I became the director of water management and planning with responsibilities for policy and planning, conservation, water resources, and environmental management. This was a key shift in emphasis because it inextricably joined future planning, environmental stewardship, and the day-to-day management of the water supply.

Presently, the City of Seattle is streamlining itself to be more cost effective and customer service oriented. Along with this drive, Seattle Water is moving towards flattening its organization and doing more of its work in a matrix environment in acknowledgment of no new resources (staff or budget). My major challenge is building a team which can continue to manage the water supply, exert project leadership, and lend consultant technical expertise while also dealing with change, ambiguity, and a shifting organization structure.

As you took on these added responsibilities, what was your staffing situation like?

I liked that job because I was able to build my own workforce through a mixture of turnover and new positions. I had the luxury of having about one third of my workforce composed of new positions. Of the four people who reported directly to me, I hired two and inherited the other two.

In my current position, I have the same level of staff in a period of retrenchment. The possibility exists that I may even lose staff if the economic picture does not stay constant and if customers stay resistant to rate increases. In that event, the issue will be how to improve our current level of work with the same level of resources. If we can't do that, then we'll need to focus on the higher priorities and identify the work we will no longer be able to do.

How were you able to use the concept of empowerment to overcome fears and enable success?

Someone said that in today's times an employer can no longer guarantee a job, but can guarantee employees' employability. As an example, in one of the many reorganizations that my department underwent, I ended up with an employee who used to report directly to the superintendent. When she was reassigned to me, she perceived it to be a demotion though she still maintained her status in the organization. In that particular case, I gave her far more exposure and more independence outside the department than she had ever had in any other situation. She gradually started to understand the advantage in the situation. During two different budget cycles I fought very hard for position requests on her behalf. I believe this also helped her a lot. Both actions gave her much more leverage. Because she had my full support, she was able to build a new network, and she eventually landed a job making a much better salary.

Tell us about your style of leadership in relation to empowerment.

Overall, I have to answer to my own values and conscience in terms of knowing whether I'm doing the right things. I've always done a lot of personal assessment. I have tried to find the balance between my social and professional commitments.

Empowerment and risk taking can be scary things. It's always a difficult call in either the volunteer or professional arenas to know to what extent a risk can be taken in allowing others to learn and stretch. With volunteers I've always been able to provide a lot more "give" in relation to standards. But with technical organizations, the standards for productivity are much more exact. How much do you let others fail when your name is attached to a project?

Given your high level of commitment and energy to your work, how have you been able to sustain yourself personally?

I have a big picture in my mind. When daily details seem to surface as more important than they really are, I remind others that this is a job. A few years from now I may be doing something different. One of the things which helps me in sustaining my personal energy is this picture of what I wish to do in my community and the commitments I'm willing to make.

When I say community, I'm including civic and professional contacts in the greater Seattle area and also commitments to people I have been close to in the Asian community. Seattle is still small enough that all of these groups of people communicate and overlap with one another. Family and a circle of close friends are also very sustaining. They tell me when I'm off course. They help me maintain a sense of balance between my personal and professional lives.

I also have long-term ambitions to run for political office. Additional challenges would probably be appealing in the future when my kids are older. It's important to me to keep the long-term picture in mind, but I don't have it all plotted down to the "nth degree."

Whenever I stretch myself it is risky because I'm not the only one accountable—what I do affects others. It is even riskier in the community in a volunteer situation because there are limited resources. In a job situation there are many challenges, but no *one* situation is singularly important. In a community volunteer situation, on the other hand, sometimes you are presented with "one challenge" that is very visible (such as a social action issue), and you live with the results for a long time. The burden is much heavier if it doesn't work. You get discouraged. Empowerment is scary for self and for others, but it has to happen or you can't get anything done.

Why have you made the choice to invest your energy in empowering others?

Because I can't do it all! It's a very practical choice. It's called self-preservation. I am a social animal, ultimately, and it's much more fun to work with other people, especially when these other people are capable. I like to think that I continually learn from them. Also, I need to hear many points of view from capable people. There are many different ways to approach a project, and the way I do it may not be the best way in a particular situation.

I have finally gotten to the point where younger people are coming to me and formally asking me to be their mentor. It's very gratifying to be asked and to think others believe I might be able to help them. I can't put a price tag on it, but it is satisfying to think that I might influence the way other people are shaping their careers and their lives.

CHAPTER 3

PHYLLIS CAMPBELL
PRESIDENT AND CHIEF EXECUTIVE OFFICER
U.S. BANK OF WASHINGTON
SEATTLE, WASHINGTON

Phyllis Campbell was born to a Japanese-American family in Spokane, Washington, and attended private schools in that community. She received her B.A. in Business Administration from Washington State University, holds a master's degree in Business Administration from the University of Washington's Executive MBA program, and is a graduate of the Pacific Coast Banking School at the University of Washington, as well as of Stanford University's Marketing Management Program. Campbell is married, no children.

She began her banking career in 1973 as a management trainee for Old National Bank. Upon completing her training, she became a branch manager and by 1981 was promoted to senior vice president and manager of all Spokane branches.

After U.S. Bank acquired Old National Bank, Campbell was promoted to senior vice president and area manager for Eastern Washington. In 1989, she became executive vice president and manager of the distribution group for U.S. Bank of Washington, and in April 1992, she was tapped to lead the Seattle-King County area. In 1993, Campbell was elected president and chief executive officer of U.S. Bank of Washington, one of the state's leading financial institutions which has about $60 billion of assets.

Active in many civic and political activities, Campbell was appointed in March 1993 as a director of Puget Sound Power and Light. In December 1993, she was named chair of "Success by 6," a Puget Sound youth organization. Campbell is also a regent of Washington State University, immediate past-chair of the Association of Washington Business, and is a board member of the Washington Roundtable and chair of the Greater Seattle Chamber of Commerce. From 1987 to 1988, she served as president of the Spokane Valley Chamber of Commerce, and in 1990 she was a member of the Washington State Growth Strategies Commission.

In 1992, Campbell was recipient of the Puget Sound Matrix Table's "Woman of Achievement" award.

☙ ☙ ☙

What would you say are the most important factors for developing an empowering workforce?

One of the most important things for me has always been making sure that my individual values and the values of those reporting to me are in sync and compatible with those within the company. It's difficult to understand the idea of individual values and corporate values being in sync, but this is the type of corporation that I want to work for.

We have six core values: INTEGRITY, CARING, LEADERSHIP, PERFORMANCE, QUALITY, and COOPERATION. The interesting thing is that we have ordered them this way on purpose with INTEGRITY and CARING at the top of the list. INTEGRITY is something we do not compromise: *We do not lie and we will not be lied to.*

This particular value is interesting because it tells the most about empowerment and about working with people. In fact, our statement of core values for U.S. Bank supports this thinking: "We care about people, our employees, their families, and our customers. We are very proud of their loyalties. We are second to none serving our communities in sharing the prosperity they have helped us achieve."

One of the things I have always felt strongly about is that one works *with* people—not that people work *for* you. You work with people and you engender their loyalty after having earned it.

This is a day-by-day job. The most important thing to me is supporting our customers, so I have always felt my job is to help those who serve the customer. One must treat everybody in a supportive manner—especially those who are supporting our customers. Because they are colleagues, I ask them, "How can I help you do your job better?" One of the things I find important is simply being accessible. Accessibility sends the message of availability when people need to talk.

Over the months I've been having breakfast with employees just to chat with the people in different parts of the company and at all levels.

So the primary purpose of the breakfasts are to give access to those who might not have access to you through normal work channels?

Yes, because when we host a breakfast, open communication and accessibility are the number one goals. It's so simple. It is just a matter of being a pleasant person. Pleasant does *not* mean, however, that you *don't* make *tough decisions*. Certainly there are challenges, but it all comes down to an attitude of saying "Good morning" to people, of showing interest in people, or remembering someone's mother is sick. These things are important. They are natural for me, but I've had people comment, "Well, Phyllis, I was having a particularly bad day, and you just smiled and said 'Good morning' and asked me how my husband was doing from his surgery. I can't believe you remember these things." It is easy for me. It is really just an attitude.

Can you give us an example of why this attitude is such an important part of your management style?

Sure. I'll use a personal example. Ten years ago I found out that I had cancer. My boss's response was, "If you have to take 90-120 days off, do it! We'll have someone cover your work for you. We'll give you as much time as you need. Just go, take the time, and get well. The most important thing is to take care of yourself and to come back healthy." I was gone about four months, and I'm fine now. These are the things you remember.

I get up in the morning feeling lucky that I have today. I know there is no guarantee of a tomorrow and you can't count on next week. It's important to make the best of what you have today, the best of every interaction, and the best of every situation. People have personal as well as family needs. Everything they are affects everything they do.

In addition to being accessible and creating open communications, another thing which is important is giving back to others. Since we get a lot from the community we live in, we need to give a lot back. To give back to the lives of others is part of the obligation. I had an early mentor who gave me great advice: "The more you give, the more you get back."

Again, investing in people is an investment in the most important asset of our business. During the week you can always give someone ten minutes to talk. Sometimes they have a career issue they want to discuss, and sometimes they just want to sit down and visit about a personal issue. If I feel I can help in that small way, then I do.

I had a caller recently who thanked me for taking the time to talk with him several years ago about a career issue. He said, "The best advice you gave me was when I asked you to tell me honestly about taking one job over another and about my skills. You were rather blunt about my skills. It hurt my feelings at the time, but now I realize that I have made different choices in my life as a result of what you told me. I'm getting a promotion because of the advice you gave me seven years ago." To be honest, I don't even remember the *specific* advice that I gave him. During this telephone conversation I just said, "I appreciate your calling" and then took the time to engage in honest dialogue.

A number of people have commented on my taking the time to talk and offer advice. I've had so many people who have done that for me that it's just part of what I now do. As my grandfather would say, "It's just part of the process of life—giving back to individuals and to your community where you can." It has now become a part of what I do naturally.

As the top executive in your organization, can you give some examples of how you handle difficult situations?

The best way to handle difficult situations is through authenticity. If someone asks a difficult question, you need to be honest—no matter what. In order to do this, it is necessary to retreat to your own values and principles. That is why working for a company that is in sync with my values has always been important to me. It is part of my own integrity. I can't be associated with an individual or a company that is not in sync with my personal integrity. Authenticity and personal honesty are a big part of this.

I have a philosophy that says there is enough for everybody. Sometimes people think promotions or opportunities should be a zero sum game. That is, if one person gets more, someone else gets something taken away. My contention is that it's not a zero sum game. Everyone can be a winner.

One of the things I've always talked to others about, myself included, is the more you give, even if it is to someone you are competing with in the company, the more it makes everybody better. I have *never* found where giving in the short run does not pay off in the long run. It eventually comes back.

Another tenet in my life is that you can get a lot more done if you don't worry about who gets the credit. As a leader you have to realize that *good* leaders are always looking for ways for someone else to get credit. If I can help someone else get the credit who has put a lot of effort and time into something, great. Good leaders step aside. I believe leaders have progressed when they are willing to do this.

Can you give us an example of how this works in your organization?

Recently I worked with an individual who championed a particular business case. I was the one who initially suggested we ought to put it forward, and I also suggested how we ought to go about it.

But this particular person actually did all of the work in pulling it together, so I asked him to present the case in a meeting. I could have presented it and saved him and me some time, but he had done all of the work so why shouldn't he get the credit. He really did a great job! Terrific, in fact! I didn't need to have my name attached to the work. This is a practical way for me to teach and demonstrate my philosophy, and it's also a natural way for me to do business.

Making that presentation provided him with practical learning and enhanced his ability to take a project from beginning to end. He was able to step forward and give the presentation and be recognized by others. People learn more by seeing and working with good leaders than they ever would in esoteric discussions where there's a lot of talk with no action to back up the words.

Individuals learn by watching good leaders. They observe things like who gets promoted and the kind of respect that is given to others. This is a very important part of developing leadership. Another part of it is having a formal management development program where specific skills can be honed by the different executives. Our management development courses provide those opportunities for executives. As good as those courses are, however, I still believe that the best way to learn leadership skills is through observing good leadership and then practicing it.

We've spent a lot of time working toward an organization with a decentralized management structure. Throughout the years we have eliminated several layers of management because we have felt that power in our organization ought to be located closest to the customer. You see a lot of this in organizations today. The more that power can be delegated to people out in the field, the easier my job becomes. Better decisions are ultimately made by those in the field because I can't sit in my office in Seattle and make decisions for customers in Spokane, or Bend, Oregon, for example.

This is a style which is perfectly in tune with '90s business strategy. It's not simply a charitable act and it's not a fad. It just makes good business sense to have people at the line level who can make 80-90 percent of the decisions since they are closest to the customer. We now have the structure in place that gives people authority, autonomy, and confidence to make these kinds of decisions.

When front-line decisions are encouraged, mistakes can sometimes happen. How does allowing for mistakes figure into the learning process?

There are going to be mistakes. I make mistakes! The only way to engender risk taking in individuals is to allow for mistakes. Leadership must tell them, "Go out and make well thought out decisions and we'll support you—even if you blow it." This is very important and a style seen in many "in" companies today.

But it's also important to discuss mistakes so that learning can take place. Discussing mistakes is a huge issue, and I know it's part of that whole hurdle of driving fear out of the workplace. It's difficult to get individuals to trust and believe when they've been raised in a hierarchical type of organization with a strong informal sanction system which says, "If you blow it, you get out or you don't get a raise." Part of the leader's job is to champion examples of people in the company who have made some mistakes. (These people should be consulted before they are used as examples, however.) The examples should demonstrate learning and should include individuals who have been rewarded despite having made some mistakes or at the least, have not been punished.

Trust is built in an organization by watching leaders. Employees learn by example and watch to see how the leader reacts when somebody makes a mistake. Seldom are the mistakes expensive, but this is also part of the investment we would have made in training. I usually say, "How could we have done this differently and what can we learn from this? Let's go forward and not make the big mistake a second time."

Can you give us an example which would illustrate this point?

A recent example comes to mind. We were getting ready to launch a major product introduction. It should have been tested out in the market in terms of presentation to customers. However, the people closest to the customers were not consulted, nor were customers. The manager of this product made the decision to introduce it without first testing it.

It happened to be a major mailing to a major group of customers. A number of mistakes were made: It was introduced very poorly, the language was very poor, and the positioning wasn't good. There were tons of complaints and problems. In some cases people even closed accounts. In any event, there were many unhappy customers out there. Part of the problem was that this individual, who is very smart, felt that he'd thought the thing through—but he hadn't. This person didn't end up losing his job, although he could have because of the cost of the lost business to the bank.

This individual was told, "Yeah, you really blew it and here is what could have been done. You could have tested people who are actually getting this product and asked for input from those employees working close to the action." This individual learned a good lesson. We half-jokingly say, "This sort of learning is the best training and education."

There are many examples in banking where people have made bad loan decisions. Even though they thought things out carefully up front, it turned out to be a bad decision in the long run. This doesn't mean we gloss over these kinds of things. We take them seriously, but we also feel they are opportunities to learn.

The thing that we don't compromise, of course, is anything to do with *integrity*. This is a given in this business. If we find anyone who has either lied or misappropriated funds, there is no negotiation. They are fired.

How do you develop a balance and an ability to sustain yourself while providing leadership to such a dynamic organization?

One person's idea of balance is another person's idea of craziness. Everyone has different energy levels. It's probably no exaggeration to say that I work an average of seventy hours a week. Everything I do requires me to be fully there. I can't just sit there and drift off. High energy is required to stay alert for twelve or fourteen hours a day.

The most important thing for me is to make sure my life includes frequent renewal opportunities. I can't say that renewal happens weekly or monthly or with frequency. Some people count on that twice-a-year vacation or the two weeks in the summer to get away. That is not frequent enough. What works for me is to spend some quiet time studying in the morning. You can call it meditation or whatever. It is time for me to gather my own energy and quietness.

Sometimes it's taking an extra five minutes before I go out the door or leaving the radio off in my car even though I'm always tempted to find out the latest news. I also exercise two or three times a week at noon. I'm jealous about this time, and sometimes I turn down business invitations, explaining, "I just need this time." So, for me, it is a combination of quiet time and personal fitness that is important. I take this time in the morning and at noon, take frequent breaks, and, of course, vacations. If I feel as if I've wasted an hour, or two, or three, in not being fully present because I have low energy, then I don't feel I have done the day justice. I need to do the best job I can. Renewal and preservation of my sense of self are important for me as well as the organization.

I often hear people say, "I'll be okay as soon as I get my vacation to Hawaii." I always think, "Wow! If I were counting on that, it would be too infrequent." Some people burn out quickly and it's important not to let that happen. A vacation once a year is not enough to help sustain the energy levels required for managing a large organization.

One day I was walking to the elevator and I was so tired that I walked right past three or four people whom I normally would have acknowledged. I was so distracted that I wasn't really conscious of them at all. This situation continued with the people in the elevator. I was simply too deep in thought and too absorbed to chat with people as I normally would have. Later, I found out that people were concerned about me. They were worried that I was sick or that the company was having problems. People read a lot into the body language of those in leadership positions.

So this is why I am aware of the importance of my energy level. Whether I like it or not, I'm being watched for those informal signals. I guess this is probably normal. We do the same thing with other leaders, political or otherwise. We ask, "What is wrong with Clinton's voice. Does he have a serious health problem?" This has been a minor lesson for me but a good one.

Can you provide us with other experiences or insights relating to empowering leadership?

First of all, as a leader you must have a vision. My definition of vision is *a preferred picture of a desired future*. As the leader of the company I still have to be able to paint that vision and then translate it so people will understand what it means to them on a day-to-day basis.

This is a journey. It includes putting together all the pieces and getting everyone to be disciples of them. It is also communication, communication, communication! You can never talk enough about the important organizational issues. Whenever I send out internal correspondence or talk on our employee videos, I always include the bank's *vision* and how we relate to our customers. It is important to communicate and reinforce these every chance I get.

Every time I go to an employee breakfast, I always start my remarks with the company vision. I let them know what we want to accomplish organizationally and that I am also interested in hearing from them. I ask for their input on how to accomplish this. We talk about what we want to accomplish, what we are about, and what our business is.

It's going to take a couple of years for me to get that message out there by talking to everybody and anybody. I get a lot of good feedback when I provide examples that allow employee stories to come alive. These stories help to champion people who do the kinds of things we want done. I can't say we're all the way there yet, but we're making progress. If you were to go out and ask an employee at 4th and Battery, "Do you know the vision of U.S. Bank?" you would probably get a big blank look. So I need to continue to "talk the talk" as much as "walk the talk." Communication is important. I need to paint the company picture continually, to give examples, and to champion employee stories.

Vision is extremely important but it's more important that the vision be communicated, translated, and championed through examples. Only then can vision come alive. We are still on that journey, and it is something in which I place a high level of importance.

Why do you think more organizations are not moving toward empowering their employees?

I guess it is partially because leaders and followers feel most comfortable with others of similar background and style of management. If the organizations they learned from tended to be top-down, hierarchical organizations and if they worked out in the past, then everyone involved assumes those kinds of organizations should still work now. We always gravitate toward what is most comfortable. I'm not saying my style is the best because there are things about my style that are more appropriate for some situations than others.

What *I'm* saying is that this style is not the only way to go. I believe in situational leadership. For instance, I'm not as comfortable with a top-down style, but there are times when that style may be more appropriate for a particular situation. Back in the '60s, '70s, and to some extent, the '80s, the top-down style probably worked the best. It has worked well in companies that are rather stable, where marching orders are pretty well understood, and where the work force is not diverse. Today, however, there is a lot of diversity in the workforce coupled with continuous change and turmoil. Empowering management works better overall in today's organizations. It is the only effective way for an organization to operate if it is serious about being close to customers. I feel lucky because the '90s style of leadership is a natural way for me to manage and is more effective in a chaotic environment. If I had spent most of my career under a different style of leadership, and it worked, then I suppose I would have used that style, too.

It's just a matter of time before the leaders who are still using a more traditional style get the message: "Wait a minute, wake up and smell the coffee! This is a different era!" Today's workforce is very different from that of the past, and if you're not able to meet their unique needs, you're not going to be profitable in the long run. Likewise, you're not going to engender workforce loyalty. Today's leader has to be sensitive. If you're not sensitive to family issues, you're not going to retain the best and the brightest. If you're not sensitive to cultural issues, you're not going to get the best of the ethnically diverse

workforce. This is a fact. Over time the message will take root,
but it's just a matter of people finally understanding that the old
style doesn't cut it any more.

Empowerment was initially known as a feminine style *only*
because many of the characteristics we were talking about
have been more typically ascribed to women, including being
sensitive, ultimately flexible, adaptable, being a coach, a teacher,
and a mentor. I also have to say that I have a number of male
colleagues within this company, as well as in this community,
who also embody this style very well. We are finally getting
away from labels. I'm seeing more of a blend now—a tendency
for people to use different styles of leadership for different
situations.

Do you have anything you would like to add to your previous comments on empowering leadership?

Sometimes I have to make a tough decision and communicate it to a group. I say, "This is what you've told me you want
to do, but unfortunately this is what we *have* to do and here is
why we're going to do it this way." This style is not exactly a
consensus-building, coaching, mentoring kind of decision-
making style. Sometimes it's necessary to tell people we are
going to do it a certain way because we *have* to. There are
certain situations in which you have to take control such as in
a crisis when you need to make quick decisions. Many individuals in the company are extremely good at this take-charge
style but have also been able to embrace the empowering
style when appropriate.

We have all learned from each other and that's what is exciting. There is now more of a blend of styles and the ability to
call on different styles where appropriate. I believe the classic
empowerment style is probably the one that is the most apro-
pos for today's corporation and organization, regardless of

whether it be a government agency or a private one. Aside from the issues of demographics and workforce composition, given all of the changes we have seen in society, empowering leadership is the most successful style for the 1990s and beyond.

CHAPTER 4

PHILIP CONDIT
PRESIDENT AND CHIEF EXECUTIVE OFFICER
THE BOEING COMPANY
SEATTLE, WASHINGTON

In April of 1996, Phil Condit took over the role of President and Chief Executive Officer of The Boeing Company. Boeing is the largest aerospace firm in the United States, one of the nation's top exporters, and the world's leading manufacturer of commercial jet transports. The company is a major U.S. Government contractor, with capabilities in missles and space, electronic systems, military aircraft, helicopters, and information systems management and has more than 100,000 employees.

Condit had held the position of president and member of the board of directors from August 1992. In that role he had been responsible for Boeing's three product organizations (Boeing

Commercial Airplane Group, Boeing Defense & Space Group, and Information & Support Services), the corporate engineering and operations functions, and the corporate continuous quality improvement function.

Previously he was executive vice president and general manager of Boeing Commercial Airplane Group's 777 Division, where he was responsible for all aspects of developing the newest Boeing jetliner: the Boeing 777. Prior to this, Condit directed all of the Commercial Airplane Group's manufacturing, engineering, product development, customer services and government technical liaison operations for more than three years.

Throughout his career at Boeing, Condit has held major assignments in sales, marketing, engineering and production. In 1983, he became a vice president responsible for the 757 Division. For his design efforts on the 757, Condit was selected as a recipient of the 1984 American Institute of Aeronautics and Astronautics National Aircraft Design Award, and in 1982 he received the Edward C. Wells Technical Management Award from AIAA.

He entered the Sloan Fellowship program at Massachusetts Institute of Technology in 1974 and, upon completion of the one-year study program, returned to the company as a manager of new program planning. He was then promoted to director of program management for the 707/727/737 Division and served in that capacity until his appointment in 1978 as chief project engineer and later director of the 757.

Condit earned a bachelor of science degree in mechanical engineering from the University of California at Berkeley in 1963 and holds master's degrees in aeronautical engineering and management from Princeton and MIT, respectively. Condit joined Boeing in 1965 as an aerodynamics engineer on the SST program.

Condit is a member of the U.S. National Academy of Engineering, a fellow of American Institute of Aeronautics and Astronautics, a fellow of the Royal Aeronautical Society, and a member of the Society of Automotive Engineers.

He serves on the advisory council of Princeton University's Department of Mechanical and Aerospace Engineering, the Executive Steering Committee of the University of Washington's Graduate School Team Certificate Program on Advanced Materials and Manufacturing, and has served on the MIT Board of Governors, Society of Sloan Fellows and the National Academy of Engineering's Committee on Science, Engineering and Public Policy, and was chairman of the Aeronautics Advisory Committee of the NASA Advisory Council. He also serves on the Executive Committee of the Council on Competitiveness.

Condit is a member of the boards of directors of the Fluke Corporation, Nordstrom, and A Contemporary Theater (ACT).

In January 1991, he was named a co-recipient of Aviation Week and Space Technology's "Laurels 1990" award for establishing a cooperative development program for the Boeing 777.

In October 1993, Condit was presented the MSOE/EAA Medal "For outstanding achievement and distinguished leadership in aerospace engineering while displaying those qualities that exemplify the spirit of the Experimental Aircraft Association and Milwaukee School of Engineering."

In April 1994 Condit received the SAMPE (Society for Advancement of Material & Process Engineering) George Lubin Memorial Award and in October 1994, Condit was presented with the Distinguished Eagle Scout Award by the Chief Seattle Council of the Boy Scouts of America.

Condit was born August 2, 1941 in Berkeley, California. He is married with two grown children.

When did you start thinking about the idea of empowerment and what does it mean to you?

It is hard to say there was one specific moment when I started thinking about empowerment. I can look back and see a number of instances along the way. The roots go back to some of my first jobs where I wanted less direct guidance and more ability to participate in discussions. I wanted to contribute and saw when given that opportunity, I could provide useful knowledge and insights.

One significant experience came from my first job as a supervisor. I had been promoted to a marketing job although I'd had no long-term expertise in marketing. I was an engineer working on the 747 at the time. People usually get promoted because they are the best at doing a certain thing. The best engineer in the structures group gets promoted to lead the structures group. The person knows how to do the structures job and the group recognizes and respects this. Promotions within the line of expertise tend to lead toward a more directive leadership style. There you are. You have the experience and expertise to tell people how to do the work. They look to you for direction. Fortunately, since I didn't have marketing expertise I couldn't use a directive style of leadership. I had to learn how to do new things and how to get this group to do what needed to be done. I had to rely on them. That was a valuable learning opportunity.

Another experience came when I was given responsibility for the sales organization. I first went around and talked to people to find out the problem areas. The answers came back, "We have too many layers of management." "My work never sees the light of day." "There is always somebody checking what it is I do." "This is very discouraging." Based on this input I made changes. I wanted to empower the employees by flattening the organization and taking out layers of management. I felt as if I'd 'freed the slaves'. I said, "You are now all empowered!" But many ran to the back of the room and asked, "Who is going to check my work?" They also accused, "You've demolished my career. Now there is no ladder to climb. My aspiration was to go up the ladder. Now there's no ladder." I learned an important lesson—*just* saying, "You are empowered" is not enough.

The final piece of my thinking on empowerment was formulated when initiating the 777 project efforts. I wanted to do things differently than we'd done in the past. I wanted to engage more people in the process. I knew there had to be better ways of increasing productivity. That's when I began to think about the power of people working together in teams. This thinking was eventually joined by others and evolved into the phrase, "working together" which is now commonly used throughout Boeing.

Would you explain the origins of the phrase "working together" and how it is currently used?

Twenty of Boeing's leaders sat down on a Saturday morning to write a mission statement for the 777 project. Prior to the meeting I had thought a lot about how I wanted things to go. I started out talking about where we needed to go and what kind of things we needed to accomplish. Out of this framework grew a brainstorming session. On flip chart pages that were posted on the walls around us, we identified the key things we wanted to accomplish and made plans for accomplishing them.

At this point one of the greatest benefits of team work happened. I can't explain *how* it happens but it always does with empowered teams. The team took my original thinking and began to refine and adapt it. They began to own the process. The project gradually belonged to all of us. It was not just mine. The statement, "*working together* to produce the preferred new airplane," was established as the mission. This statement became important to the project. We felt that no *one* of us was as smart as *all* of us together and we could produce a better product by "working together" than we could by working as individuals. This meeting was proof of that thinking.

Another word in the original statement was also important and is also used at Boeing. The word "preferred" says that the customer is the one who makes the final decision about how well the job has been done. We do not get a vote.

How were you able to sustain the momentum of this initial meeting?

These same leaders continued the meetings. We met at a Boeing recreation center called the "Oxbow" named after a bend in the Duwamish river. The group eventually grew to about 80 people and included middle managers. The meetings were free form. They all started with what we call "the view from the bridge." I got up and said, "Here is what I think is going on. Here are the problems. Here is what the customer's are saying. Here is where our challenges are."

We wanted to continuously improve our processes and productivity. We wanted to increase our learning as an organization, as individuals, and as teams. Because of this we had an outside expert come in and talk to us about *learning organizations*. We also wanted to understand ourselves and each other better so each member of the group completed a Myers-Briggs personality inventory. We updated each other on various aspects of the project and discussed problems using problem-solving, and decision-making tools.

The process was integrating and leveling. Everyone mixed together around the table. We all worked tasks together without thinking about organizational levels. We all contributed to the process. It worked wonderfully. At that point, the die was cast. We had set the stage for the future—the empowerment team concept simply took off. That was probably in 1991.

These, and other experiences are really where my thinking on empowerment has gotten its roots. I can not pin point a time when I sort of figured it out. I tried and observed different approaches. Some worked and some did not. I learned from each.

How long did it take to change management attitudes and working styles to the empowered team concept of the 777 program?

The 777 program had one tremendous advantage. This was a brand new organization. It had no history of its own. It had no turf to protect. That is really what the orientation meetings were designed to do. I learned the importance of orientation from my previous experience on the 757. We had started out with a fairly small team and were all part of the initial planning. Then people were added to the project at the rate of about 200 a week. It was overwhelming because everyone was coming over the wall with the *old* cultures. Not surprisingly, the latecomers started setting up camp just like they'd always done it before, and very soon it looked just like it did before and all the original thinking and good ideas were gone.

What did you do to prevent the same thing from happening again?

Because of that previous experience, I was determined, from the beginning, that we were going to have an orientation to communicate our beliefs and explain the working of the organization. I personally signed each invitation to the sessions. We introduced the program mission statement and the concept of "working together." Every one of those orientations had one person from the program leadership team present at the meeting. It was not a delegated responsibility. This was extremely important because many of these people had "never seen a vice president before."

Once it got started, it began to take on its own life. The words "working together" started showing up everywhere. They started showing up on stationery. That part was never planned. It just happened. You could go anywhere and say, "working together" and everybody knew exactly what you meant. They "got it." Then it took off because the process was now in gear and moving toward an end result.

We also had all-team meetings. Everybody on the program would come and talk about what was going on and review the status of the program. This was done so people would not interpret the world looking through their own knot hole; it gave them an opportunity to see a broader picture.

Were there certain team concepts that were established as the program progressed?

We had a set of initiatives. There was learning in the process. It came from initiatives such as "service-ready." This turned out to be a powerful initiative. It meant the product we were building was going to work when it first went into service. We were not going to refine it while it was in service. That was very powerful.

There was another initiative which didn't stick quite as well. It was "to have fun." I am not sure whether the culture was actually ready for it yet. It had an impact but not as big an impact as I'd thought it was going to have. Its most powerful effect turned out to be when we used it as a tension breaker at meetings. When things would get tense, somebody would inevitably say, "Are we having fun?" We would immediately feel the pressure come off.

To demonstrate the importance of the concept of "having fun" I'll relay a conversation I had with a friend of mine who is a surgeon. We'd seen the original movie, MASH together and were talking about the joking that took place in the operating room. He said this was not atypical of his experience. He said, "Think about it, how can you keep your concentration at any kind of level during a 5 to 8 hour operation? There has to be something to keep the pressure from building up—so you tell jokes."

There were many changes taking place throughout this entire program. How did individuals adapt to the changes?

I've thought a lot about the issue of change. One of the things I have concluded is that in virtually every human being's head there's a model of what the company does. They visualize how The Boeing Company works—how airplanes are sold, designed, and built. They know some pieces in a lot of detail, and they only imagine others. They fill in the blanks because there can't be blanks in the model.

Given this, when you stand in front of a group and tell them you're going to do something different, they immediately check what you are suggesting against their model. If it doesn't match, they don't respond, "Oh, what brilliance!" If the change doesn't match their model they have to go back and figure out why it doesn't match. They question, "Whose model is wrong, mine or his?" People need time to adjust to change. They need time to readjust their models. I always anticipate what the adaption rate is going to be. This is what learning is all about.

In the old work culture they had repeatedly been told, "We don't need your ideas." So they began to do creative things outside the work environment. Historically, we have sent the message of "check your brains at the door" when you come in.

Would you comment on the efficiency of team learnings and how this has transferred throughout the organization?

The original teams were called "777 design/build teams." They are now used all around the company and are called "integrated product teams," because we discovered that they addressed more than just designing and building. In addition to technical professionals, teams include finance, planning, tooling, manufacturing, product support, and marketing people.

The U.S. educational system plays into this whole subject. We have a system which emphasizes individual performance. This system tells us in lots of ways "Do not share data." We have a spelling test and everybody takes it individually. We do not get together in a team and say, "Who knows how to spell this word?" We do not take math tests as teams. There are changes, however, that are starting to take place in the educational system. Those who are thinking about these things are looking for ways to improve the system.

In addition, most people were raised to strive for good grades and high scores on the SATs so they'd be accepted at a college or university. With a college degree, they expect to be the ones who get the jobs. Likewise, our initial job assignments have that same kind of goal of *personal* achievement.

Knowledge is power. People believe, "If I know things you don't, I have advantages you do not have, so why would I want to share my knowledge? You might get credit for it." For me, personally, I can remember trying to learn *not* to raise my hand and say, "That was my idea. I'm the one who thought of that." Or, when someone who I've been working with for the last six months comes into my office and says, "I had the most amazing idea last night. We ought to do…." The temptation is to say, "What in the heck do you think I've been trying to tell you for the last six months?" Instead of saying, "Great, this is a fantastic idea. This is super. How can I help you?" you want to tell them, "That was my idea." My experience has been credit really does go, by and large, to the right places. The fear that somebody else is going to get credit for the work or that they won't be recognized for what they have contributed, causes people to withhold information or to answer only the question that you asked, not the one which should have been asked.

Earlier you mentioned some of the contradictions that occur as organizations begin the process of empowerment. Would you discuss these contradictions further?

People say, "I want freedom. I would like to be empowered."I find people believe these to be relatively safe statements since they don't *really* expect to become empowered. It is much easier to stand on the sidelines and complain, "Our leadership doesn't involve us." Many people also feel safe in an environment where they are told what to do. It's much easier to leave the responsibility for decisions with someone else. Empowerment comes with responsibility and can be scary.

When management finally decides, "We're going to let you do this," many will say, "I'm not ready for this!" "Who's going to check my work?" A circular discussion then occurs. Leadership says, "We want to go over there." Employees respond, "Yes, but you didn't ask us." Leadership then asks, "Well where do you want to go?" Employees respond, "You're supposed to tell us. You're the leader."

You can see this on a national scale. If the President queries a number of people and says, "I need input on this subject." He is accused of waffling on the topic. If he says, "This is where I want to go," he is dogmatic. I think this contradiction must exist. There is no way around it. This is a fundamental piece of how you begin to talk about an empowered culture. People have to understand that the contradiction exists.

One of the words I hate most in the English language is *blame*. Who is to blame? Who is at fault here? It is very prevalent in the media. When a negative situation arises, we look for someone to blame and then start behaving more carefully ourselves so *we* don't get blamed. Instead, we should be asking: "What can we learn from this? What do we know? What are we going to do now? How much smarter are we today than we were yesterday for having done this?" A learning approach can be empowering.

What did you observe about the willingness of the senior people to address these contradictions?

As with most large organizations, this varied a lot. There were clearly some who were ready to let go. This gets down to the fundamental issue of control. People perceive that not being in control is likely to lead them to embarrassment. Things may happen which are not quite the way they wished them to happen. The process of letting go of some of the control is a scary thing. Fear is often masked in comments such as, "Airplanes are pretty important and if we don't do this right, people could get killed. We'd better maintain control of it." We ask, "What is going to happen if we let go? Are these people prepared for this?" We adopt a parent-child relationship as opposed to an adult-adult relationship.

From a leader's standpoint, you have to be extremely careful. One small misstep sends all sorts of signals to people. If you say, "I'm willing to listen to anybody's opinion," and then you cut them short, they'll understand what that really means. If you say "My door is always open," but no one can get through, they also know what that means. When you put that against a cultural history, the missteps are even sharper because individuals are looking for them. You might not even know you have misstepped.

What changes did you personally make to address these contradictions?

I tried hard to model a very different kind of behavior. An example of this could be found in our staff meetings. In classic staff meetings there is clearly a leader. The leader takes ownership of the meeting and usually goes around the table asking staff members to show-and-tell what they have done in the prior week and also describe their upcoming plans. This process is typical of many meetings. I changed this and began using an "agendaless" staff meeting. The meetings were structured around the problems we were encountering, not about what we were doing. During one meeting, for example, one person might take up most of the time and we would talk about that particular problem. Another time there would be several different problems—not just one. Staff meetings became problem-solving meetings rather than status-check meetings. We've tended, like most companies, to be structured around control and what is going on.

Did you find you were observed by individuals who subsequently became more candid in their discussions?

Oh, yes. The "Oxbow" meetings probably provided the best example because the participants hadn't operated in this kind of environment before. Middle managers observed the behaviors of the leaders as we sat around the table and talked about all sorts of issues. They watched us and decided that this new style of behavior was okay.

Did you work with consultants during this change process?

Yes, I worked with several key players within the Boeing system. One of them was Gary Jusela. Gary is a Boeing employee who understands organizations and organizational development. He, along with Jillian Thompson, were instrumental in the planning and facilitation of the initial 777 project meetings. They have been key members of our team. During these planning meetings we used the phrase, "beginnings determine endings." This phrase stresses the importance of planning. It is still used throughout Boeing.

I originally went after Gary to work with me on a long-term basis on this project, but he was working with Frank Shrontz and was unable to commit the time I needed. Gary suggested that I use a friend of his so I hired Don Krebs. The personal piece of this is really interesting to me. Don came in one day shortly after I'd hired him and asked, "Do you mind if I sort of come over every once in a while in the afternoon and talk about some things?" I said, "Sure." At these meetings he brought in a whole array of self-analysis tools. We explored a number of areas including how I handle conflict. That was my original introduction to the Myers-Briggs personality inventory. It helped me to understand why I did some things the way I did them.

Don came in one day and said, "Let me describe something to you." He sat down and talked to me about under-bounded and over-bounded organizations. I had grown up all my life in over-bounded organizations—very structured. Everybody knew the rules. Everybody knew where the power was. But here we were running a brand new organization and doing a lot of things to keep it from getting over-bound. In the process, we'd produced a very under-bounded organization, and that situation caused a lot of fear. It was one thing to know where the underground connections were, but it was a very different thing not to be sure of where one should look for support. People can get hurt in the process. Here I was in the middle of this thing, stirring it up, and moving people around. He suggested I needed to take some time to address the structure issues.

We all have different learning styles. I learn best by talking about things. I need to interact with somebody. I want to get the author and talk with him or her. Don read a lot and we would talk about what he read. Many of the things I have "read," I've not really read. Talking with others is the way I assimilate information.

Did you include others from outside the Boeing organization in the team process? What happened?

We invited airline employees and customers into the process. This completely changed the dynamics. There was resistance to inviting the airlines in. Afterall, we wouldn't really want someone to see us doing this. This is pretty magic stuff. If they see us doing it, they'll discover we are really human beings and we don't know all the answers. We are struggling as we are learning to work in a new way, and we certainly wouldn't want someone to see us doing that. They might lose confidence in us.

When the airline employees were included, they were all amazed to find that we were real people, too. They were also afraid. They were going to help design an airplane and there were things they didn't know how to do. They wanted to solve problems they were most familiar with.

One story involves an international carrier. They had a problem with toilet seats. People would leave the toilet seats up and when the airplane took off, the toilet seats would fall down and go "bang." That noise scared the passengers because they don't like odd sounds—especially during takeoffs and landings. The toilet seats ended up being the focus of a problem-solving group. Now those toilet seats come down slowly and don't go "bang." That's an example of what the airline's employees were interested in working on. There are hundreds of those kinds of problems.

In reflecting on the 777 project, are there other aspects of the "working together" philosophy that made a difference?

We decided to allow a video group in to create a documentary of the 777 project. Our initial reaction had been, "We can't do this. This guy is going to have a camera. He's going to watch us, and when we trip and fall down and make fools of ourselves it will be on film for the whole world to see." We finally agreed to do it anyway and discovered—to our great amazement, that it wasn't really all that bad. Everybody now knows about the project, are party to it and are involved in it. All of this awareness developed because of the video. The average man or woman on the street now recognizes the 777 was built using team concepts. That's powerful.

It's interesting to watch the video now. We actually *see* ourselves for example, making a decision about the use of a particular material we had originally planned to use but were having trouble machining it. It was cracking. The whole team got together and openly documented the issues. I didn't make decisions for the team because I wanted to model a decision-making structure that fundamentally said, "You guys have all the data. You can make the decision." The cultural bias on the other hand says, "That is what executives do. We bring them the data and they make decisions." The reality is: when the data are shared openly, the answers become obvious.

Sitting on your hands and letting people debate the issues when you know what the answer is going to be is hard work. You want to help them. You understand. You've already been there. Yet, it is critical for them to go through the process. That is part of the learning.

I have watched the reverse happen when a team approach was not used. I was working with the leader of an airline. This individual had a strong fundamental confidence in his own capability. We were looking at various color medium for the interior decoration. All the materials had been set up in the board room. All the senior officers of the company were there. They worked their way around the room looking at all their options, and there was an open exchange of views. Comments such as, "This really looks good...but there are five different seat covers in this arrangement. We would have to stock five different covers in every station in order to replace soiled ones. This will require large inventories." They worked their way through the samples and focused on a design that consisted of two different seat covers.

Then the leader arrived. He went around and looked at all the samples. He took down all the information and concluded the one with the five different seat covers was the *best* one. He really thought that one was great, and he said, "This is it, this is fantastic! What do you think?" Each person around the room said, "You bet! Right on! You got it!" I knew that was *not* what they believed. The leader's wife arrived. He showed her the arrangement he'd picked out saying, "Look what we picked. This is really great. This is wonderful!" She looked at all the samples and said, "That is going to be an absolute nightmare. You have got five different seat covers, and you will have to stock all of them and keep them clean. It is going to be a mess." He responded, "Oh, I didn't see that. What do you people think?" They said, "You bet! Right on!" The force of his personality had suppressed all that good information. It can be a terrible thing to be quick and smart. The very thing that may have gotten you ahead through most of your career can suddenly become a liability.

Top-down decision making works the ego of the decision-maker unintentionally. It allows persons making the decision to exercise all their biases without necessarily knowing it. If they're wrong, then, it is difficult for them to admit it and do anything about it. It's embarrassing to be wrong. Organizational cultures continue to support this thinking.

Has your method for managing performance evolved to reflect the organizational changes?

We are in the process of doing that. For example, we have gone to what is called a 360 degree evaluation. This means we are evaluated by a number of people who have information on our performance. We have had to be careful not to let this turn into a popularity contest. It is not intended to be an opportunity for people with good scores on their 360's to get promoted. Otherwise everyone would run around trying to get promoted. The 360 is a developmental device. We ought to look at the input. Then say, "Why is it people see me that way? It's not the way I see myself." I got my lowest scores on coaching others. I had thought I was a pretty good coach, but I had to recognize this problem. I was not spending time coaching a lot of these folks so the feedback to me was, "You may be a good coach, but you're not *doing* it." We have to look at it as a development tool. It's very helpful if we do.

What were the key issues that emerged with your senior people when changing to a more empowering philosophy?

We have to personally believe it is going to work. We have to pace change. We can't simply send a memo that says, "Tomorrow you will be empowered." What does it mean to us as *leaders*, and as *people* in the system? What are the misinterpretations? A lot of people worry that empowerment is anarchy—everybody doing their own thing.

Do you use the word empowerment or do you use another word to describe the same thing?

We use it, but we are still working our way toward a common, shared definition of what it *does* and *does not* mean. Individuals in the system automatically misuse it. When a person doesn't want to do something you've just asked her or him to do, the individual will say, "I thought this was an organization that believed in empowerment. You just told me what to do." We are constantly confronted with issues of how much freedom we should allow and how much of it we should make part of the system.

We are also struggling with some issues involving teams. There's a very strong temptation to say, "If we really believe in teams, then we believe in team players. We don't want any odd-balls in the system." Contrary to this thinking, we do want some people who are outside the norm and going in funny directions. You have to have some people who are challenging the system. These teams are very diverse and are usually the hardest ones to manage. They are also the best teams.

Doesn't this get back to respect for a diversity of ideas?

Yes. But, this is difficult for most trained, educated people—certainly it is true for engineers. We are taught in school there is one answer. Therefore, if there *is* one answer and we both look at the data and get different answers, then one of us must be wrong. Since I have a fair amount of faith in the way I did the problem...you must be wrong.

As an engineer, I struggle, asking, "How can it be two Supreme Court Justices can look at the same evidence, apply the same Constitution, and arrive at two different conclusions?" In fact, this isn't very surprising at all. They gather data, process data, and arrive at conclusions differently. As in this example, we need to change our thinking from, "How is it you came up with the wrong answer?" to "Wow, that's interesting. How did you arrive at a different answer than I did?" This is a challenge to our capabilities but it can also be freeing. We don't always *have* to be right. There are often a number of alternative solutions to problems.

Do you encourage critical evaluation by providing an organizational context?

Yes. Absolutely. I want them to have the answers to such questions as: why the company is making a profit and what happens to it. I read a survey recently that most people in the United States believe companies earn a profit of 50% of revenue. I think that conclusion comes from all the "half off" sales. People think it must have cost the company only half as much as they were originally asking. They also tend to think most of the profit goes into somebody's pocket, when, in fact, the vast majority is reinvested in the company. We ought to change our accounting practices to take out reinvestment dollars before we call it profit, then pay the profit to the shareholders as a dividend. But until people understand this, they have every reason to suspect someone is making off with the fruits of their labor. We really need informed people.

Are people looking for organizational symbols? They hear the big message and then—where is the demonstration of it?

We believe strongly that symbols must grow out of the culture. They can not be imposed. An example of this is the 777 superman t-shirt. I had joked one day that it would be fun to have a superman outfit on and when the need arose, to just rip my shirt off and go to the rescue. Several of people who heard this comment decided to have fun with it. Maryann DiPasquali, who played a major role in the success of the orientations and roll-out, designed a shirt and had it made for me to wear to the next 777 orientation meeting. The front displayed a superman-type logo with a big 777 posted on it. On the back was the mission statement, "Working together to produce the preferred new airplane." The goals were to have some fun and to reinforce the mission statement in a new way. It was a huge success. It was wonderful. We also purchased teal polo shirts and everyone who attended the orientations received one. People began to wear their shirts on Friday as a symbol of team work. It was very leveling. You could no longer tell who the managers were by how they were dressed.

We also used symbols during the kick off of the 777 program. We wanted to build excitement so we created a pep rally. A cross-functional volunteer group was formed to plan this event. In the two short weeks they had to pull this together, they accomplished phenomenal tasks. Over 7,000 employees were bused to the hangar at Boeing field. The University of Washington band was invited to play. There were cow bells, whistles, footballs with 777 imprints, and pom poms. We had pep rally signs made by some local high schoolers reading, "Let's Go Get Them," "Kick Off" and "Go 777." One of our local television personalities officiated. Several board members joined in the celebration. A representative of the kick-off airline, Frank Shrontz and I gave brief speeches. It was fun and people still talk about it.

When the physical roll-out of the airplane took place we involved 113,000 people in 13 sessions. We invited 10,000 people at a time and started at 6:00 in the morning. We wanted all of the people to be involved because they had all contributed to its success.

Stories and phrases probably have had the most lasting impact in terms of symbols affecting the culture. These stories and phrases were created by the employees and continue to carry messages and define our culture. Phrases such as; "working together," and "beginnings determine endings" have been made into lapel pins, included in internal communications and imprinted onto numerous trinkets. They are important for continuing messages, creating the feeling of inclusiveness and leveling the hierarchy.

Can you speak to ways you have developed? How have you been able to personally sustain yourself?

That is complicated for me. I'm an introvert and that means I have to find some time to be alone. Following one of those sessions, I was tired. I was just absolutely exhausted and I needed to go stare out at the world somewhere. Getting away for a brief time is clearly a piece of how I sustain myself. It is important for me to be at these meetings, yet it is personally draining.

I also received some positive reinforcements during this time. There were individuals who would come up to me after a meeting and say, "That was fantastic! That was wonderful! I'm so glad we are doing this." That kind of feedback kept me motivated. In fact, we collected feedback forms at the end of every meeting. People would tell us what they thought. We had space for them to "give us a grade." At the end of meetings I would find myself reading through those as an educational piece. I would ask myself, "What did they tell us? What did they like? How could we make this meeting better?" There were always a couple of evaluations that said, "We're glad you are here." Those kind of comments had a tremendous impact on me.

You could pay me twice as much and it wouldn't change my performance one single bit because I'm already putting all the energy I have into it. This is it. This is the whole thing. I also believe deep down inside I'm affecting the lives of a lot of people. I want people to enjoy coming to work and know it's okay to smile. If that is true, then this is worthwhile.

Really smart, driven people for whom power is the fundamental aphrodisiac are going to come to a very different conclusion. I've watched some CEOs who could not let go because the job was their identity. Without the job they didn't feel they were worth anything. I know of a couple of cases where the board finally picked them up by the scruff of the neck and kicked them out the door because they couldn't let go. That's the other side.

I would always like to believe we can find ways to use human capability, the human spirit, and the human mind in more effective ways. This means we have to involve people.

CHAPTER 5

JAMES JONASSEN, FAIA
PARTNER/CHIEF EXECUTIVE OFFICER
NBBJ
SEATTLE, WASHINGTON

Jim Jonassen grew up in Grays Harbor County, Washington, and graduated from Montesano High School. He is married, with grown children. He earned his Bachelor of Architecture from the University of Washington in 1964 and Master of Science in Architecture from Columbia University in 1965.

Jonassen joined NBBJ in 1965 and established a national reputation as a health care futurist. He thinks, writes, and lectures about the future of health care, particularly as it relates to architecture.

Since 1983 Jonassen has served as chief executive officer of NBBJ, an internationally recognized firm. NBBJ is the country's second largest architectural firm and fifth largest in the world. The firm is responsible for the design of the Key Arena (Seattle), Zymogenetics headquarters (laboratories) (Seattle), Kangbuk Samsung Hospital (Seoul, Korea), St. Mary's Hospital Surgeries (Mayo Clinic) (Rochester, N.Y.), Four Seasons Olympic Hotel renovation (Seattle), the corporate headquarters for Starbucks Coffee (Seattle), and the Sun Mountain Lodge (Winthrop, WA). With offices in Seattle, Columbus, San Francisco, Los Angeles, New York and Raleigh, NBBJ had over 500 employees in 1995. NBBJ is one of the most recognized firms in the United States in publications and through its numerous design awards.

Jim Jonassen actively participates in various national American Institute of Architects (AIA) committees, including the Large Firm Roundtable, the Academy of Architecture for Health, and the Federal Liaison Consulting Group that jointly meets with the Council on Federal Procurement of Architectural and Engineering Services. He is a corporate member of the health care think tank, Health Insights; serves on the boards of the Swedish Medical Center Foundation, the School Zone Institute and the Health Facilities Research and Education Program of the AIA. He is also a member of the Public Health Group of the International Union of Architects. Jonassen is a frequent lecturer across the United States and internationally and has authored over twenty-six publications. His projects include many medical centers and laboratories in the U.S., as well as a wide variety of projects in China, Korea, and Japan.

For more than three years in a row, NBBJ has been selected by *Washington CEO* magazine as one of the "Best Companies to Work For." The following is a quote from an article, "Structured by Design," by Connie Day in the magazine, *Washington CEO* (February, 1994). According to Day:

> In the past seven years, NBBJ has more than doubled its
> revenues, which were almost $65 million in 1993 and
> it's shooting for a 20 percent billing growth rate for
> 1994. With almost 500 employees located in offices in

Seattle, Columbus, San Francisco, Los Angeles... New
York, and Raleigh, NBBJ is one of the country's largest
and oldest architectural firms ... The firm has won
nearly every design award on the books...."

How would you describe the concept of empowerment within NBBJ?

The motivation of our people (the *real* product of NBBJ), more than anything else, comes from empowering them with authority and responsibility. They want to serve society and clients and to make things happen in our physical environment. You can't motivate them without allowing them to feel a real sense of control over their own destinies. This is the major reason they became professionals in the first place. My remarks specifically apply to design professionals, architects, engineers, graphic designers, and interior designers. They are all focused on creativity. Some of the same things may also apply to the construction side of the industry but this is not directly my business so I'm not as familiar with what motivates these people.

How do you meet the challenge of sustaining individual creativity within a team?

The key is to BALANCE individual creativity with team effort. At our level of practice, there is almost no project that can be accomplished with one individual. Everyone must rely on each other to cover all the bases, but it must be accomplished in balance. Balance means a great deal for this organization. It is a word that is in capital letters. Our mission statement is to be the *best design firm in the world,* and to us this requires a balance of *design, technology,* and *process.* Some individuals are stronger in one area than another. But all of these things have to come together in balance to make a great building happen. Some organizations define being the *best* as being the best at design and the formal aspects of design. Others define it as being the best at the process of building, and still others would define it as making the best use of technology. Our view is you have to bring all three of these elements together at the highest level and in BALANCE.

Would you describe the efforts that have helped to sustain the change toward a more balanced architectural company?

The process and art of sustaining balance is ongoing, as is the creation of our approach. We think we are good, but we still struggle to improve. We have to improve the way we approach projects continuously because the environment changes and our standards continually rise. There is never enough energy to focus on everything that could be done at any one time. We are constantly reviewing our priorities and re-focusing our time on those things which we think will improve us most. We manage our efforts by (1) recognizing we must be profitable and, at the same time, (2) satisfying our clients and, hopefully, exceeding their expectations. We want the clients to come back to us with other projects. This doesn't automatically happen just because we give them a good building. If the *process* has been painful, the client may never want to see us again. We focused on this and have made significant improvements in our approach to the process since the early '80s.

What kinds of changes were made?

First we transformed the way we approach projects. We used to use an ad-hoc team approach, an approach which is still fairly common in many large architectural firms; for every new project, we created a new team. We picked the best people from the whole firm for each specific project. That sounds good, even seems logical, doesn't it? But prior to the completion of each project, opportunities usually arose for new and different projects. Again, the best team would be put together to go after the new project. But this often involved some of the same people that were already assigned to other projects. The underlying philosophy of this approach was that creative people did not need to follow the project through until the end. They were not viewed as being essential in the later stages of a project. This approach was successful at marketing our services. We were also able to sustain our work load effectively, and we did reasonably good projects.

But it was not the *best* work that we could do. The *best* work is done when the entire project staff starts out at the beginning of a project, defines with the client what that project is going to be, and then carries it all the way through to the end. This way the whole team knows, *really knows,* the project intent from start to finish and can take personal responsibility to see that the intent they established with the client at the start is reflected in every detail at the end.

To achieve this new approach, we created our studio concept. This is a concept of a small working group of architects with a complete balance of skills who would serve a client's project continuously from start to finish. We initially thought a studio group would comprise about twenty to twenty-two people. In the concept's ten-year evolution, the groups have turned out to be slightly larger, however. There are now anywhere from twenty to forty in each group. This larger size is still reasonable in terms of the need for every studio member to be up to date on everything that is going on in the studio's projects. But we feel more than 35-40 is a problem for communication. Size is also important for controlling work flow so team members can stay on projects from start to finish. The studio concept has been a major organizational transformation and has provided a focus on balance—balance of studio leadership, project leadership, and the professional growth of studio members.

How have NBBJ employees adapted to this change?

It took us approximately three years to get these changes implemented. We were fortunate in the way we did it. We had a group who was enthusiastic about the idea, and we had a single project that was large enough that it could provide the group with work for two and a half years. We had a balanced group of about twenty-two people on that project. We put them together and created the first studio. They focused on that single project with everybody participating from day one and staying on it to completion. It was a terrific experience and the job was very successful in design (it won awards), in process (it was on time on a fore-shortened schedule, under budget for the client, and profitable for NBBJ), and excellent technically. It made other members of the firm want to be a part of a similar approach.

How did the studio group make decisions and manage itself?

The project team leaders have total control of their team and its work. They discuss everything that is going on with the total studio so everyone understands decisions that are being made and what is behind each of them. Reactions of participants were initially mixed: "The change to the studio concept changed my life. It made it more fulfilling." "I wanted to do just the front end of the work and now I have to see it through." "I like to be involved in the design part and then go on to design the next project. I don't want to have to carry a project all the way through." "I'm a specialist in construction, not design." "*My* job is doing the working drawings and now we have all these designers and other people doing the working drawings."

Some people were threatened by this approach. There was some self-sorting which took place. People who really could not adapt to this total responsibility approach left the firm. Now the studio concept attracts people who like our integrated approach. It is widely known in the profession as an excellent way to practice. An effective team environment can be very rewarding. It makes each of us much better at what we are doing.

When we first created a studio, we also created a triumvirate of leadership to assure balance. This meant there was no *single* ruler of the studio. There was a process designer, traditionally thought of as an operations lead. There was a spiritual designer, traditionally thought of as *the* designer. Lastly, there was a building systems designer, traditionally thought of as technical lead. The building systems design leader is responsible for the technical aspects of both how we work and how our buildings are put together.

"Spiritual Design Leader" is an unusual title. Would you comment further on the role of this individual?

Traditionally this would have been the lead designer, the creative designer—the one who leads the vision. In many firms this role might dominate, but we were seeking balance. When we created the initial studio, we had very strong personalities in two of the key roles and a less strong personality in the third role. Our goal was to have all three aspects equally well advocated in the process. We still struggle with this balance. Persons who are good at the technical end of our work are often less forthcoming than the others. This group needs the most help in asserting leadership.

During the test period our employees continued to ask, "What does this new model mean?" "What is the studio responsible for?" At the end of the three years we had identified the studio's goals, level of authority, and its responsibilities. With the success story of the first studio, we were past the major revolution and implementation in the rest of the firm was easier. From that time forward we have continued to refine and adjust the original concept.

During the time of this major transformation to studio groups, what were the things which demanded the most energy on your part?

Spreading the vision and teaching what we were doing and why we were doing it. These activities took a lot of energy.

They were done in many ways and through a lot of all-staff meetings, studio meetings, and individual conversations. During this transition we moved into new office space in another building. This served to help the metamorphosis tremendously since the work environment was changing at the same time we were changing the work style. The new building was designed around the notion of studios. It established the open communication environment which is essential to our culture. It also created a large meeting space where we can accommodate our entire firm for stand up discussions.

Later, mentor groups were set up among the leaders of the studios. In these the studio leaders get together to deal with firm-wide issues and to share the "discoveries" of the studios. Once you have established these "essentially independent architectural practices" (in which studio groups can be viewed), internal competition is created. This is largely positive but can become negative if carried too far. The mentor groups counter the negative aspects by encouraging a sense of sharing and mutual support.

The first mentor group was the process designers. Their issues were thought to be in the most immediate need of help at the time. Focusing on just one group's issues was a mistake to some extent. When one group's issues are emphasized more than the issues of other groups, a mind-set is created which believes that "one group's issues are more important to this firm."

After working with the process design leaders, we felt we had a reasonable handle on the *process* of doing our work. Our next focus was to raise the level of design quality of the product. We could not lose the quality we had achieved in process, but we needed to raise the level of design quality also. So, we created a design leaders mentor group.

The last mentor group we created was the building systems design group. We now believe we should have created it earlier. If we had, we could be five years further along in achieving balance by now. We created this group three years ago. They have needed to understand they are truly on a par with the other mentor groups. The logic and symmetry of having all three groups in a formal mentorship structure across the firm was not initially seen. It was thought the principals of the firm would provide enough cross fertilization. We were wrong. Now that we have all three mentor groups it seems so obvious that all were needed if balance was the goal.

As we have continued to refine, we've gone beyond even this triumvirate of leadership. We later changed to a quadrumvirate of studio leadership, and it now includes the marketing/client relationship function which we call communication design. This is one of the aspects of studio life. Again, it is an important link in what this profession and business is. We want everyone to learn enough about the profession to have the capability to become a partner in the firm. They must have an understanding of the marketing aspect as well as technical, process and design. Adding marketing mentorship to the studios allows the staff to participate in and learn this aspect of practice as well.

There are some aspects of our approach that are very compatible with the Japanese approach to a work team. We have a partnership with a Japanese company. They have an office here in our Seattle facility, and we have an office with them in Tokyo. We've now had a year of interaction with them. There are a lot of similarities in the way we approach things as a team. When you believe everybody who touches the product should have responsibility and authority for the product quality, it is very close to the way Deming taught many Japanese to work. That is one of the things which has made us compatible with our Japanese partner.

How did you educate team members to become more knowledgeable about NBBJ?

Let me go back and cover how this has affected individuals and what we did to reach the individual with the message. In the initial period of trying to change the process, there was a great deal of discussion at the firm level, at the studio level, and at personal levels. A lot of that involved me, but a lot more of it involved other advocates for change. It was easy to see who had an understanding of what we were doing and who were becoming the champions. Fortunately, my partners have always been a key part of this. The real secret to success is the commitment of the entire partnership. This is a whole story in itself, and we've been very fortunate in that regard.

One of the things I did personally was to demystify the financial performance of the firm. Working with our chief financial officer and business manager and using my own experience in managing projects, we did an analysis to determine what it takes financially to make us successful and what can also be controlled by project teams. We simplified this down to four things people can easily understand and influence successfully. They are *chargeability, multiplier, receivables,* and the *cost and success of marketing.* Each of these is also easy to measure. So if each team and studio understands these and plans their work effectively, we will do well.

From the beginning of our cultural shift in 1983, we have openly shared how we are doing financially, so the staff are always aware of the status of the firm's profits. We explain our operating margins, how the money flows, how it is used to sustain the company, and why we have to get better than we are. We share all of that with staff and, for the most part, they appreciate being party to it. They understand their influence on the bottom line and know how it affects them personally.

Initially, we spent a lot of time talking about the financial model and studio concept. The good side of this was it demystifies company finances and builds credibility. The staff now believes we are all in this together and can all influence the bottom line. The down side was that the initial emphasis on finances created a feeling among some people that finances were what we cared most about. This is one of the problems when trying to achieve balance—you feel you've got to over-emphasize in one area to bring it up to the level of the others. But it is read as an emphasis which goes well beyond just bringing the problem into balance. It is often read as "the thing that is most important."

How have you achieved balance between leader-initiated change and individual autonomy during the change process?

It is a continuous struggle with the big "B" word, BALANCE. It's a constant tug between achieving the right level of leadership and the right level of self-autonomy and group autonomy. It changes from time to time as the issues change. I feel much of what we now do as an approach and most of our policies of operation were initiated by individuals thinking up better ways of doing things and sharing them. But there are always some individuals who are at odds with an organization's basic values and beliefs.

There are some situations where a "benevolent dictator" really has to make changes in personnel. In the past I have taken responsibility for most of this. I listened to opinions from many people but I made the final decision and acted on it. It is my hope that as this team environment and mentorship approach matures, more of these issues will be self-correcting by people recognizing on their own they are not a good match for this work environment. This has happened already to some extent.

As we speak, it is my feeling the time is right for the leaders of several studios to advise one of their peers about role changes which could improve their performance, but so far I have not been able to get them to take the bait. I think they've been ready and have even wanted that responsibility. They've made recent basic policy decisions about operations, and this tougher peer mentoring is a logical extension of that. I think it could be done well in the context of that group which is supposed to be suggesting ways of taking the firm forward—yet they haven't crossed this line at this point. This is a good example of a balance point. I'm ready to have them do more than they seem to feel they are ready to do.

Ultimately there does have to be *a* leader. But the real issue is, how much can leadership be shared? How many people can participate in leadership before there is no leadership? On the one hand, you can't simply decide you are going in one direction and then just hand it over the fence, particularly in a challenging group of professionals. But we still don't know the point where everyone is so participatory in leadership that direction loses clarity. As a leader, you've got to be deep in the trenches with dirt all over you along with everybody else or you'll have no credibility in this kind of creative, challenging environment.

Do you have any other lessons from the above process, any recent experiences which have helped you to become more aware of the need for individuals to communicate their feelings in relation to their work?

Let me give you an anecdote. Recently my studio had a semi-annual retreat where the studio members set the agenda and talked about issues which were of most concern from their perspective. Two people stood and said they felt that they had been treated badly in the studio. They had been released from one project team and put on another team. It was obvious the communication on the change had been handled poorly and, in fact, one of them had found out about it from a third party. This led to a discussion about individual abilities and work preferences, independent of studio needs. The lesson it brought home was a clear need to better define how this studio operates, what its needs are, and the limits on feasibility to accommodate preferences in project assignment. It also reminded us of the absolute necessity for clear, direct, and rapid communication of decisions affecting people's status.

One of our goals is to try to enhance career opportunities for people. This has always been an issue for the studio. In a small group you understand where everybody is in their professional development, and you can help mentor them and accelerate their growth. We do this reasonably well, but there are obviously limits. This is an issue which has not been talked about enough. Expectation levels are high because of our openly-stated organizational values.

This raises the issue of running a team, studio, or firm as a democracy. It can't be done. Yet, expectations are set up in a system that says, "You all have a say in what you do, including responsibility and authority for the quality of the product." How do you achieve an understanding of the BALANCE of what is possible versus what is not? The only way this can be achieved is through positive experiences over a long period of time. Issues also need to be dealt with openly, talked out, and a core of meaningful, long-term values established. Some issues can be addressed as policies, written or unwritten, but it is the basic values, established over time, that are the most meaningful.

Would you reflect further on the issue of personal autonomy and sensitivity in a democratic organization?

The best answer I have found to that problem is the "magic of communication." You have to have communication in any successful culture. When someone sees something that seems wrong to them or inconsistent with what they have heard, they get upset. This needs to be talked through.

A discussion in our recent retreat centered around the value of the "lean production" concept in this firm. How do you stop "the project assembly line" to talk about feelings and perceptions? You can't just push a button because there is no mechanical assembly line here. Yet, it's just as important for us as it is for a manufacturer to "stop the line" and fix anything which is not working.

To address this, we created a stick with a flag and bells attached to it. If something needs fixing, you grab that stick and shake it. We all stop what we are doing and talk about what is going on. It has been used twice in six months and has created very positive solutions to important issues.

We also bring in outside professionals to help create positive interactions within a project team that is going to be together for a long period of time. We are doing this on a project now. The job has got to be done fast. The schedule will have incredible, unrelenting pressure for six months. Even with this tight schedule, we took half a day at the start to discuss individual communication styles and differences. By doing so, everybody understands each other better in terms of the way each communicates. On a job like this interactions can become quite heated with different opinions and a lot of pressure. When this happens, people are reminded there are legitimate differences in communication style. For some, tolerance for slow speakers and indirect communication is hard to come by, but identifying it as a legitimate stylistic difference up front helps.

In our profession communication skills and tolerance may be more important than in some others because design schools taught us a negative approach to critique. Most of us were taught to create something, have it put on the wall, and have it criticized. Criticism at school had a tendency to emphasize what's wrong rather than what's right. We try to help people change through training and dialogue about behavior and communication techniques which are appropriate, and we focus our critiques on an exploration and comparison of ideas and alternatives rather than attacking ideas.

What do you see for the future of NBBJ?

Clearly we feel we are progressing toward our vision of being *the world's best design firm*. But to assess that, we talk a lot about other perceptions of us. We also talk a lot about where we are headed and how it relates to the rest of the world. In looking for new challenges, I have to admit that I tend to be very much excited—if not influenced—by the last thing I have read. I often preface discussions with my studio by saying, "Here is the latest thing I've read and here is what I see in it." So there is a lot of discussion about what is happening globally in relation to changes that are needed in society. This is helpful in order for all of us to understand our own change in context. If we decide to change internally, it really doesn't mean much unless it is complementary to the direction the world is headed. I think these discussions are helpful in that regard. Our staff generally think they hear the straight story in terms of our firm's commitments, and they feel a part of the process of strategic exploration. Specifically, we are currently globalizing our practice, most aggressively in Asia, and seeking some specific new building-type expertise in markets we see as having high future potential.

As a personal note, seriousness and drive can scare people sometimes, so I recognize that I'm not always the best person for communicating issues. Our partnership is great because I've got a partner whose personality balances mine. He is much more easy going. We share message delivery. A strength of this firm is the balance of people at the top who have different skills and personalities *and* have great respect for each other.

Tell us more about the firm's partners and the nature of their shared decision making.

There are seven partners who hold equity in the firm and assume all of the liability. Of the seven current partners, all but one came from within. That one came through a merger. The issue of choosing a partner is really a critical issue which is not just a matter of qualifications. Qualifications get you to the table, but the ultimate decision factor is compatibility. This is difficult to define because compatibility could be viewed as a group of people who are narrow in focus, who all think alike and are unlikely to challenge each other. This is not what we want and it's not what we have. We want people who can work together, respect each other, bring different perspectives, and advocate their views in a strong, positive way. This is the key to the future of the firm.

Here is how our selection process works. Every year we re-examine the future of the partnership. We use a model which looks at where each current partner will be in his or her career and what additional strength the partnership will need. It includes a number of factors that support internal growth opportunities for our staff.

I was made a partner when I was still fairly young. I think it was very good for the firm to have a different generational perspective. We are careful not to overlook younger candidates, and when the circumstances are right, we will reach down a generation because a certain individual has the right stuff. We are also concerned about BALANCE. We're seeking to achieve a better gender and ethnic BALANCE. We're encouraging internal development of both.

An example of other partnership decisions is the creation of regional offices as studios. These studios have been created to reach out into different regions of the country. This allows us to have a locally focused practice with the advantage of a national skill base. A lot of work that we do requires sensitivity to local values which come from regional educational systems and are related to regional environmental issues. All of this is important to a successful practice, and we can be better positioned if we have strong studios in each area in which we practice.

We have created several regional studios: San Francisco, Los Angeles, Raleigh, and New York. The partners take responsibility for strategies for further growth and continuance of the firm, each regional office, and each building type specialty. I would also like for other layers in the firm to have a say, but these are decisions that can't be decided by everybody. The group with the ultimate overview is the one who ought to make the decision, and that is the partners. Carrying a studio or a building type specialty that has not been performing well for a long period of time can seem like a real burden to some but may seem like an important long-term investment to the partners. Ultimately, my partners and I have to make the final decision.

These are typical of the level of decisions made by the partners. Similar decisions relate to pursuing international opportunities. When we are faced with difficult decisions, the questions we ask include (1) How much money are we willing to risk for what kind of return, and (2) how much do we invest in the future? Ultimately these decisions *have* to be made by the leadership. All staff should be aware of the issues and understand the thinking behind them. Their opinions matter, and they should also be voicing them. They are an important influence on the decision.

Could you give us an example of a decision which will be made by the management which requires input from staff members?

There is an issue being considered currently which will test the boundary between the partner and the mentor group. This decision has to do with the way profits of the firm are distributed. In our current system the principals have contract ownership of some of the profits of the firm. In addition, there is a performance bonus system in place at the principal level which also includes a few other key employees. There is also an associate program which has a bonus tied to it, and there are studio bonuses which are based on both firm-wide and studio performance.

The current re-examination was initiated by a couple of principals who felt that the relationship between the rewards to principals and the rewards to the studios was out of balance in favor of the principals. Now they are re-looking at the bonus systems. The motivation of the principals is a key issue for the partners and the financial rewards are an important part of that.

The motivation of the two principals to give more to staff and their alternative suggestions are a very reasonable challenge to the status quo. I have told them I will support any decision which is reasonable, but I reserve the right to veto it if I think it will unbalance what we are trying to do overall. I also told them I would talk this out with them before I would veto it. So this is an example of one decision where I'm not willing to say, "You've got it. Go ahead and do it." I'm willing to give them a lot of leeway because I think what they come up with may have merit. This judgment is a key part of what makes leadership work or not work.

You have placed a high value on respecting the knowledge base of your employees. Could you discuss this further?

A recent book I read is *The Work of Nations* by Reich. The thing I find interesting in it is the issue of what we really have to sell. Reich emphasizes that in an information economy, or company, the capital resides in the brains of the people. What this says to me is that the whole issue of stewardship is absolutely enlightened self-interest. This is not just a matter of being a better way to run a company, it's the only way for this kind of an organization to survive. Our staff have the *knowledge,* and whether we like it or not, they have that creative thing that we are selling. This is especially true as we get better at what we do. We have trained people to understand what makes us as good as we are, and it is not difficult for them to walk across the street and do the same thing.

Reich is suggesting we look at ourselves in the cold light of day. All we are, all we have is what resides in the *hearts, souls, and brains* of our staff. If they do not feel valued, if they don't feel they own their destiny, they will walk.

Our studio teams have got to see their future here as their best future. For that to be true, we've got to achieve what we've said we want to achieve. *We've got to be the best.* What is the biggest motivator for our people? It's not money. It never has been. It is association with things which make them proud, that make them feel they are special, and they are achieving what they went to school for and are making a real contribution to the environment. We have to be the *best* for our people to feel this is where they want to be and, therefore, everything they learn, think, and do is used to improve the practice here.

It is a tremendously exciting time in all aspects of society. I think it is particularly true in our profession. It is true because it is changing rapidly. It is changing because of global market pressures and because of technology. It is changing because of our understanding of human relations. Every industry we serve is also changing tremendously. Our problem solving and interaction with our clients teaches us a lot about ourselves.

Clients tend to confirm for us that we bring a lot to them. Part of this comes from the richness of our experience, as well as our primary skills. When you are working with seven or eight industries at any one time, you see in detail a lot of what is happening differently in those industries, and the ideas that you glean can cross fertilize both what we do for our clients and what we do for ourselves. With the kind of people we have here, there is rich soil for ideas to grow.

Given the energy you have invested in developing the creative potential of others, how do you sustain yourself on a personal level?

I think more than anything it is the notion that *we have the real possibility of being the best.* This sounds abstract, I know. What does it mean to be the *best* and why do I care? The fact is that I grew up with the notion and was trained in school to want to be the *best*—to want what we do, what I do, to excel, to

absolutely be the *best*. Combine this with the fact that we create real things. We build things you can walk around, and see,
and will exist for a long time. This is like an aphrodisiac!

I can't articulate it well, but there is something powerful about
going back and seeing something tangible that you have done.
On the one hand, you have a sense of pride about how good
it is and at the same time a sense of disappointment at how it
might have been better. There is an assurance you can constantly make what you do better and better—and there is the
possibility of being absolutely the *best*. Your building can be a
source of joy to people for a hundred years.

But what influenced me most, I think, was my father. He was
a builder, a good one, and concerned about his craft. Watching
him instilled within me a lot of concern and joy for doing
something well. That is my earliest, and still the strongest, influence. He was selfless in his attitude about the importance of
doing something well for someone; this was more important
than any other aspect of a project—including making money.
This set of values has probably influenced me more than anything else.

Because of his interests, I remember always having building
publications around our home. I encountered Frank Lloyd
Wright's work (which has influenced a lot of people) in *House
Beautiful* when I was a teenager. That hooked me on architecture. These are the things that make me want to do what I do.
They are the most powerful things I can think of in my
experience.

One of the things which has given me and my partners a
great deal of satisfaction are the encounters we have had with
great people—people who are still a part of us, those who
have left us, and the many great and interesting clients we
have had. All have been very positive experiences. Even people
who left us because things didn't work out between us have
ended up great friends. In most of these cases, they have gone
on elsewhere and have done extremely well. There is a great

sense of satisfaction in knowing we have had an influence on the profession by being a training ground for, and an enabler for, other professionals' successes.

Chapter 6

TOMIO MORIGUCHI
Chairman of the Board and Chief Executive Officer
Uwajimaya
Seattle, Washington

Tomio Moriguchi grew up in the Seattle area and graduated from Garfield High School. He completed a B.S. in Mechanical Engineering from the University of Washington in 1961. Moriguchi is widowed, with two children: Tyler, a graduate of Wesleyan College, and Denise, a student at Bowdoin College.

He worked for the Boeing Company for about two years before joining the family business. Since 1962 Moriguchi has been with Uwajimaya which was established by his father Fujimatsu Moriguchi back in 1928 in Tacoma. Uwajimaya is the largest food-related business owned by Japanese Americans in the Pacific Northwest, with retail (Seattle and Bellevue

Uwajimaya stores), wholesale (Seasia), export (Uwajimaya Trading), manufacturing (Kustom Foods), and distributing (Food Service International) divisions and other affiliated companies such as Sun Luck and NikoNiko brand items, FSI Alaska, Magic Dragon, Town & Country Travel, and others. He held a variety of positions in the family firm, became chief executive officer (CEO) and president in 1965, and after serving in that capacity for over 30 years has been recently named Chairman of the Board. Uwajimaya generates over $60 million in annual gross income.

Moriguchi is civic minded and committed to bringing improvements to the International District and Asian community. He actively serves in more than 40 organizations and has received numerous awards and recognitions, including the Japanese American of the Biennium award by National Japanese American Citizens League. The U.S. House of Representatives recognized this award and directed that the award recipient be noted in the congressional record. As a businessman he was given the 1992 Western Washington Entrepreneurial Success Award by the U.S. Small Business Administration. In May 1993, the Small Business Administration (SBA) recognized him with the Region X Entrepreneurial Success award. He has also received the Seattle Community College's Volunteer of the Year; North Seattle Community College's Distinguished Businessman and Founder of the College; and International District Rotary Club's International Citizen of the Year award. In 1994, the House of Representatives of Washington state passed a resolution honoring Tomio Moriguchi for his contributions to the local community and the state.

He has simultaneously served in leadership capacities as a director, president, or organizer of over forty-five professional and civic organizations. Some of those include original founder of Nikkei Concerns (formerly of "Issei Concerns") a non-profit organization administering the Seattle Keiro Nursing Home, which currently serves 150 patients. He is founding member of the Japanese American Chamber of Commerce; director of the Pacific Science Center; president of Japan America Society of the state of Washington; vice chairman and a director of Seattle Alliance for Education; director of Leadership Tomorrow; past chairman, Advisory Board for the International Trade Institute of North Seattle Community College; director and past vice president of the Greater Seattle Chamber of Commerce; past president, director of the International District Improvement Association; past treasurer of the Puget Sound Private Industry Council; and member of the Community Development Roundtable.

How would you relate the concepts of empowerment and control to a family-owned business?

True control is when you can fire somebody. You can't fire family members, so you really don't have true control. Philosophically, I believe in empowerment. Empowerment is a natural way of dealing with a family culture. In our situation you have no choice. You *have* to empower them.

Do you feel that organizations with a family culture are similar to other organizations with empowered workforces?

In any organization you must have honest respect for other people. This should be practiced regardless of whether the employees are family members or not. People will invariably surprise you with their positive responses if you demonstrate that you feel good about yourself and them—but most of all—demonstrate that you trust them.

Empowerment systems develop over a long period of time. Sometimes you end up badgering people in certain situations, but if you continually communicate the organization's vision so they can see where you are going, they will continue to move forward.

In addition to building trust and continually communicating the vision, what other leadership components are critical to initiating and sustaining an empowered organization?

You can't empower people unless you give them information. You can't even be on the *same page* unless you share information. To be on the *same page*, the other person must have basically the same information you have. If you are honest, you don't need to worry about sharing "inside" information. If you are honest, you don't even need to worry about sharing tax issues—or even—what your competitor finds out about you.

It is important to understand that sharing information is not a bad thing. It comes about naturally when you take responsibility, through delegating to others, in your organization.

Would you describe the employee reward systems at Uwajimaya?

First of all, we believe we should share the wealth so we have a profit-sharing program, and everybody benefits from it.

About 15 percent of our employees participate in a program called the Goal Achievement Program, or GAP. These employees negotiate performance goals independently with their managers. The system works a little differently with each position. Percentages can vary, but basically, each position is broken into three, not necessarily equal, compensation components. One of these three compensation components is related to *company* performance, another to *work group* performance, and another to *individual* performance.

This process of setting performance goals encourages a freer flow of information. It is actually required in order to agree on goals. The negotiation process that leads to the completion of the GAP plan is vital. It is a good tool to find out if the employee and manager are really thinking the same way. If not, our experience shows us that two people can usually keep talking until they both understand the overall plan. If joint understanding is not achieved, the person may be reassigned to another area.

Family members who are owners take a long-term view of personal compensation. They do not establish large wages for themselves unlike some family-owned firms. They don't take wages over $200,000 or drive fancy cars. Employees have a sense that the owners are fairly compensated in relation to themselves. I don't mean to say that employees dwell on compensation issues for family members, but they have a sense of fairness.

What is the familial organizational structure of Uwajimaya?

There are seven siblings in my generation. Six are in the company, and five of the six are in senior management. One sister prefers to be a buyer. Since senior members of the first group of siblings are nearing retirement, we have become involved in succession planning.

Among other things, we are considering a change that would allow us to lead and to manage the business at two levels. There would be an Ownership Board to provide the organizational direction and leadership and an Operational Group for day-to-day management.

How will succession planning guidelines be established?

There are nineteen nieces and nephews in the next generation. Our challenge is to change some of the traditional Japanese business practices that were followed by my father. In that system, the sons inherit more than the daughters. Assuming this first generation moves on to retirement in the near future, the system would be very unfair and would create disparity for the next generation. We have discussed these issues in family meetings, and we have also hired an industrial psychologist as a vice president to help us with these issues.

What kind of employee training exists within the Uwajimaya company?

Out of 340 employees, about forty-five are in the GAP program. This program provides training that has been negotiated between employee and supervisor and is specific to the needs of the position.

All employees are also involved in other training programs. We have a vice president for human resources and a formal human resources department. We need staff specialists now and are working on training programs that are appropriate to these needs. We have formal classes for sales, sexual harassment, communication, and other issues.

As an organization, we also feel a need to address societal changes. We work at staying up on current societal issues. We believe that if we don't, these issues can, and will, come back and bite us.

How is empowerment essential for sustaining a long-term leadership role?

Empowerment is being lazy a little bit, too. You realize that you can't do it all yourself and that you have to rely on other people. Delegation is a "calculated trust" that needs to be developed between the employee and the manager. When you delegate, you need to believe the other person can do it. They also need to have a chance to prove they can do it. If you delegate something to someone, you can't be constantly thinking, "I wonder if this person is doing it right?" You should set the parameters and then not get too involved in the details. There might be ten ways to do something. You can get so wound up in details that you drive everybody crazy. A lot of delegation happens intuitively. Part of the judgment comes from working with people and knowing them well enough to trust they can do the job. If the success, or failure of the person doesn't hurt the bottom line, the person in charge needs to let go.

Would you give an example of this?

Not long ago two employees felt they needed private offices. I felt they would probably do better if they were together so they could back up one another's work. I felt locating them together would tend to support those connections. Despite my feelings on the matter, I let them make the decision but asked them to think it through and justify it to me. Part of my ability to empower others to make decisions is based on my understanding that the family will back me up. Family decision making has to be democratic, and I always need to know how far I can go while still having the backing of the family.

Do you have any other comments regarding your ability to sustain long-term organizational growth?

For me, the time in my life dictates the priority of succession planning. It's not an easy issue to deal with so we have obtained outside professional help. We recently developed an Advisory Council to the Board of Directors. The Advisory Council is composed of outside experts in their respective fields, including large-scale retail development and operation, nationwide restaurant and bakery development and operation, and family-owned enterprise, non-profit and community legal representation. The council is charged with providing independent and professional counsel to the board in the areas of long-range and strategic planning.

The people I look up to, respect, and try to emulate are those people who run good businesses and also try to develop a global picture. Uwajimaya has had good success partly because we spend time supporting other organizations that are connected to our customers. My father always said, "If you are going to give money away, give it to organizations where the youth are—that is where the future is."

There is never enough money, but we try to be good neighbors in the community. We attend hearings for the city council, we write letters about issues affecting our community, and we participate in many neighborhood charities such as United Way. We also support educational institutions such as the University of Washington, the Seattle Community College District and the Seattle High School District. We take these issues seriously.

We feel good about participating in them, and they help to establish good public relations.

Participation in community activities also provides a useful network that can give an accurate picture of how the organization is viewed in the business community. It also provides many antennae for feedback. Feedback about your business that comes from a network of community groups is clearer than the feedback you receive from just one customer who might be unhappy. Networks can also bring issues to our attention. It is good business even though the return may not be measured on a dollar per dollar basis. We have found comments from other community leaders to have substantial merit.

Could you give us some examples of how your employees participate in community outreach?

We probably could do more, but we do have a bi-weekly communication flyer. We don't try to "toot our horns" too much but ask our employees for information on their church or youth groups so we can help in supporting them. Giving to other organizations is a good investment, and it's important to give with the right attitude. If you give grudgingly, it's not fun for the person receiving or the person giving. The sad part is you can never do enough. It's difficult to keep a BALANCE between corporate profit and corporate giving, but the BALANCE is necessary.

CHAPTER 7

NORMAN RICE
MAYOR
CITY OF SEATTLE
SEATTLE, WASHINGTON

Two-term mayor Norman Rice, the youngest of four children, grew up in Colorado and attended public schools there. He moved to Seattle in 1968 to attend college, earning a bachelor's degree in Communications and a master's in Public Administration from the University of Washington. He is married and has a grown son.

He was elected mayor of Seattle in November 1989 after serving eleven years on the Seattle City Council. He was re-elected to a second term as mayor in 1993 with 67 percent of the vote. Rice is the first African American mayor in Seattle's history and one of the first African Americans in the nation to become mayor of a city with such a small African American population. His current term expires at the end of 1997. In his leadership role, Mayor Rice serves the needs of a diverse public constituency in the greater Seattle area.

During his second term, Rice is continuing to build on Seattle's economic strength, environmental quality, and cultural diversity to meet the challenges of the 1990s and the coming century. Among his top priorities are (1) revitalizing Seattle's public school system and ensuring a quality integrated education for all students; (2) recognizing and promoting diversity in city government and the larger community; (3) investing in Seattle's economic and human infrastructure; and (4) continuing his efforts to reduce crime and violence through strong law enforcement, crime prevention efforts, social programs that address the root causes of crime, and community mobilization in partnership with traditional law enforcement methods.

In addition to his work as an elected official, Rice has been a leader in countless Seattle community groups and civic efforts, including assistant director of the Seattle Urban League, director of Government Services for the Puget Sound Council of Governments, president of the Mt. Baker Community Club, and a member of the board of directors of Planned Parenthood of King County.

In June of 1995, Rice became president of the U.S. Conference of Mayors, a national, non-partisan organization that represents cities with populations of 30,000 or more. The role of the U.S. Conference of Mayors is to aid in the development of effective national urban policy, strengthen federal-city relationships, ensure that federal policy meets urban needs, and provide mayors with leadership and management tools of value in their cities. During his 12-month term as president, Rice has emphasized an agenda of a nationwide campaign for greater tolerance and respect for diversity, restructuring federal programs to reduce costs and increase effectiveness, real federal tax reform that encourages economic development and job creation, real welfare reform that addresses the causes of poverty, including job training opportunities, and building stronger alliances between cities, counties and other local governments nationwide.

Rice has emerged as a national spokesperson on the challenges and opportunities facing America's schools and the nation's urban centers.

Have you always been an empowering leader or have there been turning points in your evolution?

I have not spent a lot of time thinking about this, but in retrospect, I would say there were probably several turning points. To begin with, I am the youngest of four children. This has clearly had an impact on my life. I like to say that I wasn't spoiled, or at least, I was spoiled differently than the others. As the youngest, I was forced at an early age to be in a sharing mode. Our family was not rich so I learned to give over many of my wants to my older siblings. I also learned that I don't always *need* everything I think I want. For me, this was a giving type of relationship. I also discovered, early on, that sometimes by giving a little you get a lot in return. This usually worked better than asking for everything directly. I learned that when my parents saw I was willing to give, they treated me differently, and as a child the rewards were great. So the roots of that aspect of my philosophy go all the way back to my childhood.

In addition, my mom and father divorced during my childhood. This also gave me a compelling need to want to make things work. I wanted to make the home environment better because divorce has such a wrenching impact on a family. I was thirteen at the time, and in order to keep stability, I became a kind of negotiator. I was not a problem child or a great student. I was outgoing and I always had a lot of friends. In these friendships I was never dominating or authoritarian and always allowed others the freedom to be themselves. I developed excellent networking skills and soon became a leader during my school years.

Tell us about your early schooling. How did your educational experiences affect your future?

I always had a broad spectrum of friends and was never tied to any one particular group. I was elected to student body offices in junior high school. Then in high school I changed from a predominantly white school to a predominantly black school. This was a significant change. I ran for office my first year at the new school and came in last. At that time I vowed I would some day become president of the student body—and I did. Once again, I understood there were different sectors and groups. I learned the importance of networking and became better at it. Even though I was not very handsome and not a very great athlete, I was many times named the one "most likely to succeed," and "most likable."

When you reached college level, were there any changes in the nature of your school experiences?

I went to college and flunked out. At that time, the university I attended had a very closed environment for socialization and involvement. The university social structure was built around the traditional Greek sorority and fraternity system. There were probably only about thirty blacks out of 15,000 students and most of them were athletes. All the school organizations were Greek-oriented, and at that time, they didn't allow people of color to join. Consequently, I found my outlet through parties with other groups and ended up failing.

How did that situation affect your life over the next few years and toward the future?

It was devastating. I flunked out of school! Flunked out— didn't drop out—*flunked* out. Because of this, I stayed out of school for the next five years. During this time, I worked as an orderly in a hospital, a meter reader, and finally, as an engineer's assistant at IBM in Boulder. I always had a desire to go back to school. I thought about it a lot but didn't know when I would eventually do it.

While I was out of school, I started acting. Acting is also a sharing and giving kind of thing because when you act, you are part of a team. You have a role to play, and you play that particular role well. But you don't try to over-dominate in your role with others. In acting, everyone else has a function, too. In the end, it's very rewarding because when you do your job well and others do their jobs well you all get applauded by the audience. If you don't do your job well—or if any element of the cast is weak—you get taken to task by the critics.

It was during this time that I started thinking seriously about going back to school. I was acting the night Martin Luther King, Jr. was assassinated. We were scheduled to perform *"Raisin in the Sun"* by Lorraine Hansbury. When we heard the news, we were in shock. We met at the theater and talked about what we should do—should we perform? Should we cancel the show? We elected, as a group, to go on in his memory rather than turn the lights out. There is a line in that play that says, "It seems like God gives the black man nothing but dreams, nothing but dreams." We all looked at each other at that instant and just broke down into tears on stage. I think at that point in time, I made a decision that I wasn't going to dream anymore—I was going to *do* some things. So I got my life together and came out here to go back to school. At age twenty-five *I literally started all over again*.

How was your philosophy of leadership affected by your move to Seattle?

I went to Highline Community College, did well there, and later transferred to the University of Washington where I got a degree in journalism. Part of my journalism experience took place while I was working for a radio station as a reporter while going to school. I was lucky because I was able to continue expanding my personal networks during this time. Then in graduate school I studied public affairs. While at the University of Washington, I also worked part-time for the Seattle Urban League.

By this time, I was involved in the kinds of things that would lead me into politics or into community service. I was actually in more a public service mode than a political mode at that time.

To backtrack a bit, I didn't realize until recently that the situation in my high school probably mirrored more what the world was *going* to be for me than what it really *was* at the time. Even though my world was predominantly filled with black people, there was a large Hispanic population and a large Asian population; whites were really a minority in my school. So I had a heightened sense of multicultural awareness and inter-action—it was an excellent foundation. But this made it even more difficult when I went to college. We had all gotten along in my high school. It was a rainbow. Unfortunately, that rainbow didn't seem to exist anywhere else in that state. Only afterwards did I realize how lucky I had been in high school.

In the '70s, I became assistant director of the Seattle Urban League. I also went to work for the Puget Sound Council of Governments. This was a collaborative group of people coming together to forge a vision for the entire urbanized area of Western Washington. I went from there to working in a bank in the corporate contributions area. This was a great job because I got to help other organizations give the bank's money away! Again, I was able to enhance my negotiation skills as we worked to develop win-win situations. When people came to me with proposals that we knew we couldn't fund, I would work with them to adjust their programs so they would fit with the bank's objectives. The negotiations were very positive and rewarding because everyone was a winner.

It sounds as if your networking and negotiation abilities have helped you a lot in your career. What have you learned as a result of this?

I've learned that you can't win without really *knowing* the other person. I'm a very personal person and I like to know personal things. I'm not a business-only type of person. As I'm talking to you, I want to know what your family is like. I want to know about your kids—what makes you live and breathe versus an all-business discussion. I like openness, and I like honesty. I can't lie well. If I have to withhold, then I can't be open. I try very hard never to get in a situation where I have to withhold information. I really believe in the concept of sharing, so what I have to offer is what I am and where I am.

Could you describe the development of your career in public service ?

I really started tracking toward a career in politics about the time I married Constance. We have a wonderful, warm and loving relationship. Constance and I have one child, a twenty-three year old son who is in graduate school at the University of Washington in the transportation planning department. Prior to UW, he graduated from Eastern Washington University. He's been a great son and we're very proud of him.

Kids of politicians or "famous" people sometimes have it harder, but he's an athlete and has created his own niche growing up. I think that has kept him grounded. He got rewards and gratification from his own exploits rather than living in the shadow of his parents. It can be a heavy burden for some kids. He's been an all-star in football and in track. I never did anything in sports, so he's never had to compete with my past. I never lettered. I am not an athlete at all.

At the time Constance and I were married, I became president of the Mt. Baker Community Club. I realized in a community club that you couldn't be authoritarian, especially in a non-paying kind of situation. Team building was the key in this environment. I also was elected to the City Council where being a team player was key. After many years on the City Council, it was time for me to move on, so I ran for mayor in 1985.

What did you learn from the mayoral race?

I think I may have moved away from the empowering mode because I thought, "This is what the public wants from me." I ran as sort of a neutral person who would not be offensive. I think I lost that race for a number of reasons, but probably the main one was that I was trying so hard to please people that they couldn't see where I was with my feelings and compassion—what I stood for. I ran for what I *thought* the people wanted and I was wrong in that approach. But I learned a good lesson.

Then in 1988 I ran for Congress and lost. We knew there was a good chance we were going to lose when my opponent [Jim McDermott, a long time state senator and three-time Democratic candidate for governor] reappeared on the scene after being gone from the area for a period of time. [McDermott had left politics briefly to work for the State Department in Africa but returned to run for Congress in the summer of 1988.] But I was comfortable with myself in that race and, even though I lost, I think I actually won in other ways. As I talked about the needs of the city, I also talked about myself from a personal standpoint. I think that helped people get to know me better. I need to say, however, that losing is not a warm thing. After losing both the mayoral and the congressional races, I thought seriously about getting out of politics in '89.

But as the 1989 mayor's race began to unfold, there was a very divisive anti-busing referendum on the ballot which was really polarizing the community. I said, "You know, we need somebody to hold all of these groups together. If we believe in this thing, we'd better step up and do it rather than complaining about it!" So I jumped into the race at the last minute—but not without a wealth of supporters. After I'd won the election we started bringing representative people together to help shape the direction of education, its priorities, and emphasis. We wanted it to be value-driven rather just another policy exercise. These kinds of meetings made a real impact on everyone.

They felt they were finally represented by a stakeholder who really cared about and understood the workings of their part of the community. We held dozens of meetings and got people talking. We showed how we could take their basic themes and bring something substantial back to them. They began to value our understanding and advocacy.

In the end, a comprehensive plan for revitalizing our schools emerged from our dialogues with the community. This kind of open approach has been really positive. We're now implementing this program and we are starting to see results in the services to our children, the support for our classrooms, and even in academic achievement. I don't know if there is one best way for making changes, but making value-driven decisions is the method that works best for me and really gets at the core of who I am and how I like to work.

When you talk about the activities that you are involved in, you always say WE instead of I. Can you explain more about the empowerment of your administrative staff? How are they rewarded for their efforts?

This is one of the most difficult issues in government because we don't have a merit system in which monetary rewards can be given. It's an important issue that deserves more attention. Since we've not been able to grant monetary rewards, I've been working on methods for giving people status. Part of this is accomplished through assigning leads to important projects and in providing opportunities for deserving individuals to "shine in the sun."

You know, some people aren't comfortable with empowering others and letting them shine. The other day I was asked if I was worried about the popularity of the new police chief, Norman Stampfer, since everyone likes him so much. I'm definitely not worried, rather I'm proud of him and hopeful that people know that the mayor had chosen somebody really good for that important role. You should have smart people working with you, and you should let them shine. You've got to give them opportunities to stand out and to give them the credit for their successes.

It's important to say "Thank You" to staff members—pick up the phone, send a personal letter, and do the kinds of things that people don't expect. I wish I had money to compensate them for their extra efforts, but as you know, money is not really the primary driver for most people anyway—it's recognition. A lot of our general fund departments can't offer monetary rewards either, so they have also found innovative ways to appreciate staff. Managers walk around more to look at and talk about current projects, and to say "Thank You" for previous projects. We've implemented a lot more city employee recognition programs than in the past.

As mayor I work very hard to be accessible, even though at times I feel as if I'm not as accessible as I'd like to be. I hold walk-through tours and town hall meetings all across the city. These are important personal interactions which help to eliminate the layers between me and the public. At the same time, all departments in government need to be able to do the same thing. I think the biggest challenge I have as a manager is an unwieldy management structure. I have close to thirty department heads, which doesn't allow me to have the intimacy that I would like to have. I am working on changing this.

What would you say are the key ideas that are critical to sustaining the long-term growth of a community or work group?

The main thing is that you've got to be in tune with your values and be willing to stick to them. If your values are changeable, you're going to have a hard time. I believe in consistency. Because I'm a linear thinker, I have to go from A to Z and not take shortcuts. I believe in building open programs so people can see how they are doing. You can't come into them in the middle and expect the same level of understanding. I think this is what empowerment involves—building from the ground up.

You have discussed a very open leadership style which requires high levels of energy. How do you renew and sustain yourself on an ongoing basis?

I am a sensitive person. I like poetry. I like literature. I am eclectic, and I don't have any real heroes. My mother and grandmother were strong women who influenced me in very profound ways. My "outgoingness" is probably from my father, who was a wonderfully warm, funny person whom everyone liked. He was gone from the family a lot, but he was well liked. The most sustaining thing for me is having a consistent philosophy. You can't change your philosophy in midstream. If you get a new philosophy, you're in conflict with a whole lot of things. I think I'm far more religious than I probably outwardly show. I believe in the spiritual being and a sense of God, and although I'm not church oriented, I believe in an ultimate God.

When I'm tired and have free time, I go on vacation as one method for renewing myself. On a day-to-day basis, the biggest thing that I do to sustain myself is to be able to laugh. I think a sense of humor—the ability to laugh and never take myself too seriously—is an important renewable force in my life. I really do. I've said, "If I ever stop laughing on this job, then I've got to leave." To be mayor, you have to love it, like it, and laugh about it. Every day you have to see something about it that is fun. There has to be a genuine love for what you do. If you lose that, you won't be an effective leader and you can't empower people. It is finding value in the minutes and moments that you *have* and putting time into your life to enjoy it.

CHAPTER 8

JAMES SINEGAL
PRESIDENT AND CHIEF EXECUTIVE OFFICER
PRICECOSTCO, INC.
KIRKLAND, WASHINGTON

Jim Sinegal is president, chief executive officer and a director of PriceCostco, Inc., which was formed in 1993 as a result of a merger between The Price Company and Costco Wholesale Corporation. The company operates a chain of cash and carry membership warehouses that sell high quality, national branded and selected private-label merchandise at low prices to businesses purchasing for commercial use, personal use, or resale, and also to individuals who are members of selected employee groups. PriceCostco has over $19 billion in sales, more than 257 warehouse clubs in operation, over 25 million cardholders, and in excess of 60,000 employees throughout the United States, Canada, Mexico, United Kingdom, Korea, Saipan, and Taiwan.

Sinegal co-founded Costco in 1983 with his partner Jeff Brotman, 10 years prior to the merger with The Price Company. Before that he was President of Sinegal/Chamberlin & Associates, a firm acting as a broker and sales representative for a variety of food and non-food products from 1979 through January 1983. From October 1978 through August 1979, Mr. Sinegal was executive vice president of The Price Company, and from February 1978 was vice president of Merchandising for Builders Emporium, a chain of retail home improvement centers. In the 23 years prior to 1977, Mr. Sinegal held a number of administrative positions with Fed-Mart Corporation, a discount retail chain, the last of which was executive vice president in charge of all merchandising and operations. Mr. Sinegal has 40 years of merchandising and operations experience in the retail mass merchandising field.

Through the years he has supported a variety of educational and community service organizations. Current commitments include serving as trustee for Seattle University and as a board member for Zion Preparatory Academy. He has served in a variety of positions for United Way of King County, including chair in 1994, and is currently an active board member. As chief executive officer of PriceCostco, Mr. Sinegal supports corporate giving for the Fred Hutchinson Cancer Research Center, Children's Hospital, and for scholarships for city and school programs.

Mr. Sinegal is married and has three grown children.

What were the early influences in your education? How did you get started in this business?

I grew up in Pittsburgh where I attended a parochial school through the tenth grade. We then moved to San Diego where I finished high school. I went on to complete two years at San Diego Junior College and later attended San Diego State College.

I started working in the retail business when I was about eighteen years old and still attending San Diego Junior College. I began as a will-call clerk at Fed-Mart and over the next twenty-three years worked my way up in the company. I then felt that it was necessary to make a change and decided to start a discount retail business like this one. When the economic timing was finally right, I found a compatible partner, and we started a business. Jeff Brotman and I are still together, and he is currently the chairman of the board of our company.

When Jeff and I first met, I had been in the process of talking with people about various communities in which to do business. Then Jeff and I formed the partnership and we continued looking for potential business sites. We felt Southern California was too competitive and that other communities, such as Dallas, Denver, and Chicago, would be difficult communities from which to recruit people. Jeff was from the Seattle area and knew the community. It met our criteria relative to the competitive environment and the ability to recruit people, so we decided to stay here.

How did the idea come about of starting a business based on the concept of offering discounted prices on quality items?

We established the business as a cash and carry for the owners of businesses. We recognized that these people were typically at the top end of the demographic scale and so it made sense that they would want *good* products as opposed to poorer quality ones. The key here is *value* as opposed to a cheap price. Our intention, with everything we do, is to give value.

What type of people were you looking for as you hired your first employees?

The first people we hired were additions to the management team so we were looking for people who understood this business. Specifically, we were looking for people who understood the business of mass merchandising, of giving value to the consumer, and had developed that type of expertise over years. Many of the initial hires were people from Southern California. I had worked with them for many years and knew their capabilities. We hired a couple of people from the Seattle area, but of the ten initial people, eight of them came from Southern California.

We also wanted to deal with people we liked and who were compatible, industrious, intelligent, bright, and had integrity. We specifically looked for these things and had discussed them prior to making job offers. This is very important when you're starting an organization. You're dealing with those people every day so you should be dealing with people you can trust and like.

This business is not "genetic engineering." If you get individuals who are bright, they can be taught this business very quickly. There are some intuitive aspects to it and there are some art forms—but it's not complicated.

Would you describe how you and that first group of ten people initially got started?

We had already established a business plan. We knew what we wanted to do, and we knew we wanted to concentrate our efforts in the Northwest. We didn't know for sure whether we would expand beyond the Northwest so we focused our efforts between Seattle, Portland, Spokane, and Boise. We anticipated there could be possible opportunities that might present themselves beyond the Northwest, but for our initial planning we restricted our thinking to that area.

We initially raised enough money to start three units. In 1983, we opened the first one in Seattle in September, the second one in Portland in October, and the third one in Spokane in December.

By the end of that first year I would guess we probably grew from the original management team of ten to somewhere between 350-400 employees.

Would you describe how you oriented and trained new employees during this period of rapid growth?

Jeff and I set out to hire 10 good managers who could take on the total responsibility for their areas. The individual who was hired for marketing did all of the marketing training, and the individual who was hired for operations did all of the operations training, and the merchandisers did the merchandising training, and I trained those ten people. I told them, "Here is what we are going to stand for. Here are the parameters of the business. Here are the number of items we're going to carry. Here is the pricing structure. Here is the refund policy. Here are the wage scales." As a team, we then went through and detailed each of these areas and taught them to the individuals who were charged with performing the work.

In the final analysis, management is the management of people—pure and simple. I know it's not possible for me to do everything so I attempt to teach them to do things as I would do them if I were there to take care of every customer, stock every shelf, ring every register, sign up every member, or write every purchase order. I teach people to do the work in just that fashion, but I know they're smart enough to figure out new ways which are even better. The sum of these people is certainly brighter than I am by far.

We have trust in the people we hire. No one person can get us into trouble or destroy the company, but we all have interdependent parts that we play. We have checks and balances in the system that don't allow anything to be done by oversight.

We are working with "razor thin" margins, and I mean "razor thin." We can't tolerate big variances. This means we're all in this together. We use the expression, "For things to really go wrong, we have to screw up in unison."

A typical retailer will always have shrinkage. Shrinkage in our business is "unexplained loss." For example, you start off with $100 worth of inventory. You later take account and discover that you now have only $98 left. This means that you just had 2% shrinkage. The missing 2% is unexplained. You don't know what happened to it. You could have lost it in a whole assortment of fashions. It could have been lost from bookkeeping, theft, miscounts, or markdowns that were not recorded. In any event, it is unexplained.

Managing shrinkage well is the mark of a good management company. As a matter of fact, many people in the retail business will tell you the quality of the management team will be determined by how well shrinkage is controlled. We control ours to an unbelievable percentage. We run shrinkage that is in the 2 tenths of a percent range. Some of our competitors will run ten times that—2 percent to 3 percent. There are companies who run as high as 8 or 9 percent. When working with our kind of margins, we can't afford to go beyond our current levels. We have to pay attention to detail but at the same time trust the people who are working for us.

What is the selection process you use for hiring new employees?

It would be extraordinary for us to hire a senior level person from outside of our company. We take the attitude that 85% of the positions in our company are going to be filled internally. This is another way of saying that 15% are to be filled from the outside. We believe it's necessary to have some influx of new people into the organization for vitality and change of view.

As a matter of fact, I can't remember the last time we hired an officer from outside the company, other than an attorney and an accountant.

We promote most of our warehouse managers from within the company. In those instances when we do hire from outside the company, we look to organizations that we know are good organizations and have the values that we believe are necessary in our business. Then we take them and train them. We don't make them a manager until they've gone through at least a six- to eight-month training process.

Can you describe how this works?

It is an on-the-job training process. We put newly hired employees in the warehouse working alongside one of our current warehouse managers for several months. We take them through the buying office. We give them a total exposure to the company, but they spend most of their time working right with our managers in the warehouse—doing the jobs and seeing how they do the jobs.

In general, I believe any manager who is not spending at least 75% of her or his time teaching, including orientation for new managers and long-term staff development, does not understand what the job is, and I mean this sincerely. Teaching is not necessarily done in classroom sessions—most of the time it's done by example. If a manager is walking through the warehouse and sees a piece of paper on the floor, he or she should pick it up. This is a teaching process that is ongoing, and management involves teaching. This is the biggest single portion of a manager's job. Every now and again we have to call a time-out and stress the importance of modeling good management practices because we're not getting the utilization of the entire workforce. We're trying to get people to do the job the way we understand it is supposed to be done. Hopefully, new employees will do it that way and find new and better ways of working smarter and improving processes. Most of them have an enormous enthusiasm and want to do well.

If you want to get a message like this across to a large organization, the message has to be straightforward and it has to be relatively simple. You can't make it too complicated, because that can become a shortcoming. Many times we make our businesses more complicated than they really are.

Do you also send employees to outside training?

Most of the training happens internally, but we sometimes send people to outside classes. Most of these are specialty-type courses such as tax classes, computer classes, and job enhancement courses.

How was this new type of business initially perceived in the retailing community? How did you promote the concept?

One of the things we recognized early on was a certain amount of skepticism about this type of business. When we opened down on 4th Avenue South, people commented: "Here's this big warehouse with these fork lifts running around." "They're charging a membership fee to shop here." "They've got this stuff stacked to the ceiling." In addition, people ask, "How are they getting all of these brands?" "What's the mystique here?" "What's the catch?" We decided we were going to take all of the "catches" out of the process.

As an example of what I am talking about, when we tried to apply for a liquor and wine license we were put through the ringer. We were asked every question imaginable, and the questions got way out of the context of liquor and wine and into things like how we were going to price milk and what we were doing in many parts of our business outside our beer and wine department. This experience taught us a valuable lesson. We concluded that, "We're always going to be under this type scrutiny. People are always going to be questioning what we're doing because we do things differently. They're always going to ask: 'Why don't you advertise?' 'Why do you charge a membership fee?' 'How can you get this merchandise at these prices?' 'It must be seconds.' 'It must be irregulars.' 'There must be a catch to it.' 'There's no guarantee.'" So we decided that we were committed to running the business in a fashion that takes away all of these objections by offering a refund policy and a warranty on the product. This is better than any place in town.

We also decided that we were not going to advertise. We were going to put the merchandise out and let the customers choose for themselves. We were not going to mislead customers in any fashion, and we were not going to employ high-powered sales people who would try to switch the customer from one product to another. We would let the customer make the choice. We were not going to take credit cards, and we were not going to do a whole myriad of things that we considered not to be cost effective.

How did you communicate the values of the company?

In the course of doing this, it became essential to teach our people in this same fashion because this process becomes duplicated many times through example. We've always told employees they don't have to worry about doing anything dishonest for our company because dishonesty—will not be tolerated. They should always do the right thing and most people's judgment is pretty clear on what that is. They don't lie to the customer and they don't misrepresent a product. They know they shouldn't sell an inferior product nor buy an inferior product. Everyone should be honest in every aspect of the business. We know we're going to be under a magnifying glass because the very nature of our business makes people wonder, "What's the catch?" We've got to convince them there *is* no catch. We have always been subject to more questions and scrutiny than most other retailers.

Would you talk about the merger between Price Club and Costco Wholesale Corporation? What were the implications for cross-training from one company culture to another?

We had different cultures, but fortunately they were closely aligned because many of us had worked together for years and had established the same sense of values. There was as close a match of cultures as you could get in any merger, but nonetheless, there were some variances. We re-stressed the "marching orders" to all the people: how we were going to run the business, how we were going to accomplish our goals. It became a consistent teaching process.

Many of the new people had to learn specific business practices such as the refund policy and the maximum-mark-up philosophy. On an ongoing basis, they had to go through issues that were more philosophical than functional. There were some people who were at odds with how the company should be developed. Wages at Price Club had been lower than those at Costco, so we had to gradually bring Price Club people up to the higher wages. Our view has always been if you pay the people good wages, you promote greater productivity. We continually examine our reward structures.

Now that the merger is complete, how would you describe the operating principles of the company?

We wanted to build a company that was going to be here 20, 30 or even 50 years from now, not a company that was going to be here for the short term. We felt this as an obligation, not just for our employees, but for our members, our shareholders, and our venders. All of them have a stake in how well we do. Our decisions are based on this understanding. We try not to make short-term decisions that can destroy and undermine our philosophical culture.

After years of business, people trust us because of what we represent. We have customers who come in and think, "If

PriceCostco sells it, it must be the right price." It takes a long time to build that trust. You don't want to give it up. You want to guard it very selfishly. You want to make sure that you understand and value this and ensure that everyone in the organization also understands this value and that one wrong deed can destroy and undermine a big portion of what has taken years to build. Once you have lost customer trust you'll have to "fight like hell" to get it back.

How do these operating principles impact employees?

The same thing is true with employees. If they think a manager of the warehouse is dishonest, then it's easy for them to conclude they should be dishonest. If we constantly preach what the values are and no one lives up to them, employees quickly get the message that our values are meaningless. We have to be consistent, and this is part of why teaching goes on continually. We also have to monitor this continually. Our charter is a very simple one. We believe that our obligations are to obey the law, take care of our customers, take care of our employees, and respect our vendors. If we do these four things, in essentially that order, we'll accomplish what we ultimately want to do, which is to take care of and reward our shareholders. We always aim to conduct the business in that fashion. It's a simple concept.

We have a lot of faith in our people. We assume people are worth keeping and are worth giving a second chance. Any employee who has been with us for more than two years can't be terminated without the approval of a member of the company's senior management team. This is unusual. This is how much we believe in the people we hire. We want for them to have confidence that they have a job. We want them to know they are not subject to the whim of someone who is having a bad day. We believe that if you hire good people, give them good jobs, and pay them good wages, then good things happen. We will continue to run the business on this basis.

You are continuing to grow internationally. What have you learned in that particular arena that you would like to talk about?

It is fascinating. International business is the greatest learning experience of all. We started doing business in Canada about ten years ago and we initially thought, "What is the big deal? Canada is only 140 miles up the road." We found out what the big deal is. It's a different country with a different currency, different language, and different laws—everything was a big deal because we had no Canadian expertise. At first we stumbled along. Learning to do business there took us a while and it was a humbling experience. Once we learned how to do the business, we were very successful.

These challenges took place in a country located only 140 miles from Seattle with an almost invisible border, so you can imagine the new issues we found when dealing with Korea, Taiwan, United Kingdom, Saipan and Mexico. All of these have been very challenging opportunities. We had to first get an understanding of the particular country and then be prepared to control our own destiny. We believe that we need a partner in each country. We had to gain an understanding of the specific culture and get a sense of their unique set of values. We don't want to do something improper in any country, either with the government or from a cultural or social standpoint.

How does the concept of empowerment and trust transfer to other cultures?

I don't know if I have any answers to that. This is one of the reasons that doing business internationally is so challenging. Things move so fast. For example, would anyone have dreamed that 5 or 8 years ago companies would be doing business in most of what used to be referred to as Third World countries? There are large numbers of people in many of these countries and some of them have money to invest in business. This means there are many opportunities for expanding globally. But there are also many issues to sort through, such as vast distances and different cultures and languages. We're going to have to work our way through every one of these issues, but we won't sacrifice our company values. We'd rather not do business in a culture that's not a good match for our style of business.

The retail business is a tough business. Discount retailing is even tougher. It is just slightly tougher than "defusing bombs." Because of this, we have to make the business fun. It has to be something we want to do because in some instances our general managers work 50, 60, or 70 hours a week. We had better be enjoying ourselves, taking these challenges one at a time, and hanging on to our values. We are consistently translating these values in the various countries where we do business. They are so basic: Take care of your customer, take care of your employees, and respect the members you are doing business with. These are pretty easy to translate.

Sometimes our international partners are nonplussed by us as we stumble through these cultural transitions. They occasionally have a much more chauvinistic attitude toward their employees than we do in the United States. It takes local managers a while to get used to using first names for all levels of associates. On the other hand, the associates usually find it very refreshing. They like it and grasp it quickly.

After a period of working together, have you found that the principles of empowerment transfer to the cultures you have worked with so far?

Oftentimes I think more is made of cultural differences than is actually there. People are the same—they want to be empowered. They want to know what is going on and they want to participate in making the company better. They want to be recognized for what they do. They want to have an opportunity to have security and to grow.

Whether you are working domestically or internationally, it's a matter of really recognizing what it is you want to do, having fun at it, and recognizing that you can't do it all yourself. You have a lot of people you count on and you have to trust them or "you're never going to get another night's sleep."

Organizational leaders invest a lot of energy into running and growing the business which leaves them little time for personal renewal. Would you talk about how you continually sustain and renew yourself?

There has to be some balance. I don't think I have as much as I should. You have to understand that you can't work every minute of your life even though you're consumed by the business on an ongoing basis. I value my family and the people I love. I want my children to love me and I want to continue to be friends with them 20 years from now. I want to know that I can talk with them and I want to know that we respect each other. I've seen too many examples of people who become extraordinarily successful at business and extraordinarily *unsuccessful* in their personal lives. I don't want this to happen to me.

CHAPTER 9

DOUG WALKER
PRESIDENT
WRQ (WALKER, RICHER & QUINN, INC.)
SEATTLE, WASHINGTON

Doug Walker is a founding partner and the president of WRQ, a Seattle-based software company that employs more than 500 people and topped $100 million in sales in 1995.

In 1981, Walker and four partners founded WRQ which makes PC software that connects personal computer users to enterprise computers and information networks. WRQ markets its Reflection® software in more than 50 countries throughout the world. According to *Soft-Letter*, WRQ is currently the 16th largest PC software maker in the United States and according to *Washington CEO* magazine, WRQ is the best middle-sized company to work for in the state.

Walker is also an active volunteer and supporter for numerous community groups. In 1994, The Nature Conservancy presented Walker with their highest individual honor—the Oak Leaf Award—in recognition of his work for the Conservancy and environmental conservation.

Originally from Greenville, South Carolina, Walker graduated *magna cum laude* in mathematics from Vanderbilt University in Nashville, Tennessee. He later moved to Seattle, Washington, to attend the University of Washington's graduate school of mathematics.

He is married, with one daughter.

You are one of the original founders of WRQ. How was the company organized?

When I moved out here, I was 21 and my wife was 19. One of the things that interested me about Seattle was that I had heard it was beautiful—and it was—and is. I have always been interested in the outdoors so a lot of my social acquaintances in Seattle were in the climbing community. In fact my current partner, Craig McKibben, is a fellow I've worked with for close to 19 years. We met because we were both climbers. He is the one who first suggested I get into the computer business. I ended up working in the same place he was working. I learned how to be a computer programmer and computer consultant on-the-job.

Then a few of us actually decided to form this business. In fact, McKibben was not in on this original step because he had committed to a big expedition to the Himalayas, and it wasn't good timing for him—so he came in later. We started this business because we wanted to start a business. We didn't have specific ideas at that time. I think we probably have some marketing materials that make us sound more organized. But the truth of the matter is we figured we could probably make it in the computer business. The thing was to get together as partners and then figure out what to do.

At that time I had very little background in the computer business. I had received my undergraduate degree in mathematics from Vanderbilt University.

When we started the business we had three programmers and a marketing person. This was a good way to start because frequently technical people are too focused on the technical side to think about the business and marketing issues. Having this diversity of types right at the beginning was fortunate.

Initially, we were able to support ourselves with consulting and contract programming, but our ultimate goal was to create products. We tried 3 to 4 different product ideas, but it took several years before we came up with one that worked.

So the three original partners were Walker, Richer, Quinn?

We also had a partner named George Hubman. Everybody is retired now except McKibben, as mentioned earlier. McKibben joined us a little less than a year after we started the partnership.

Originally the four of us did everything, the programming, the marketing—everything. We gradually started hiring additional staff. We hired one or two people a year between 1981 and 1986. We did very well with contracting and consulting and we were always profitable. All along we continually threw out new product ideas to see if they would work. Then in 1983 we came up with combining communications work that we had done with some PCs. This was a hot prospect. In about one year's time, as the product began to do better, we switched all of our efforts to that product and phased out the consulting services. We actually started selling the product in 1983.

The company has been fortunate to have a monotonic trend. We've always done well and kept up with business trends. In recent years our growth has been in the 30 to 35 percent a year range.

This company is a little different from a lot of high-tech firms because we didn't have a product when we began. We couldn't get financing. We had no ideas. When you're trying to get a venture capitalist, they like for you to have a plan and a product. You can't just say, "Give us some money and we'll figure out something. Trust us." The original capitalization of the company was $125 per partner and that is still our total capitalization. It really is. That is all the money we have ever invested or brought into the company. So on that basis, the company has always had a pretty good financial performance.

How long have you been in this location and how many employees do you currently have?

We've been at this location since March of 1994 and we have approximately 525 employees.

How did you move from the initial focus on programming and marketing to the leadership model you are currently using?

I've always tended to hire people on a peer-type basis—not exactly like a law firm, but kind of like that. I have a very participative partnership style, and we've always tended to choose pretty senior people. In other words, we haven't really had a theory on leadership. People have always asked, "Where did you come up with this current philosophy for operating?" I respond, "Well, I don't know. Let me think of something."

People sometimes give us advice. They say, "You've got a lot of chiefs at WRQ, but you don't have many indians. Don't you ever hire peons?" We don't believe in hiring peons. It would be boring.

What are the key organizational elements at WRQ?

WRQ is in a funny place. It's a distributed organization, *not* a top-down organization. Some people like this and some people don't—even within our own organization. Some people want personal authority and meaningfulness in their job while others prefer a clearer sense of direction. They want to be told definite boundaries. I find that some people think more defined organizations represent extremely well run businesses.

There is a lot of ambiguity at WRQ. Our approach is not universal. We tell individuals, "We are giving you the responsibility, now go do some stuff." They say, "Great! What should we do?" We respond, "We don't know exactly. Develop something useful, important, whatever that might be." We try to hire people who prefer this style.

What is the most common job for which you recruit?

The most difficult and competitive jobs are the technical positions such as programmers. These are the highest demand jobs.

How would you respond if one of these programmer's came to you and said, "I've heard a lot about your organization and how you encourage people to work independently. How does this really work?"

A lot of programmers are used to working in isolated, heads-down environments. We would warn them that we don't operate that way and give them a sense of how we do work. We have a team-oriented, cooperative environment and this has negatives for some people.

We would also tell programmers that we expect them to have a very global outlook. This means they are expected to pay attention to marketing and business issues and to dedicate a portion of their time to visiting customers and even looking at support issues.

I really want the programmers to be influenced by the customers. They have to talk to the customers. They have to get the whole story. They won't be able to make global decisions without it. If the customer calls and I actually talk with her or him about the details of a problem, then I think the problem is *very* interesting and *very* important. I'm susceptible when my personal reputation is on the line—everybody is. The problem doesn't have the same sense of urgency when the information is passed on rather than received firsthand.

If you're going to have distributed decision making, then the key element is accessing information. Business schools teach that a traditional hierarchical organization has a vertical flow of information. If you are trying to build a more modern organization, you have to get rid of the hierarchies. You might have an organization chart but you want to have a network model for your information flow. That requires a lot of input and talking and interacting.

We do share our philosophy with potential new employees. They need to understand that they'll have to supply much of their own direction. There are some people who are weak in this respect, but it is the strength that is needed in *our* environment.

And do some people self-select out at this point?

Oh, yes! They realize this environment is not what they are looking for. They prefer to work on pure technical issues and not get "dragged" into the other aspects of the business.

We try to recruit people who are pretty well developed in both the human and the technical side. We have to, otherwise they won't be happy and neither will we.

We don't have an adversarial interview process. Some companies do. It's a good thing for them because the adversarial interview fits with that organization's environment. But if you don't like the interview process, there's a good chance you won't like the company. In the end it's a good self-selection process.

All of the team members are included in the interviews. This makes them more committed to accepting the new person. Likewise, the new person also has the chance to get more in sync with the team members. This reduces the typical first-day initiation hazing process. New employees start the first day here with a built-in advocacy. The team knows that if the new person fails, it's mud on the *team's* face—*not* the new employee's. We're committed to this interview process. It gives everybody a forum sort of feeling.

We have a reasonable reputation for being a "nice place" to work, but it might not be "nice" for you. That's why we're very careful to let people know what to expect. Just being a "nice place" is not good enough. There are a lot of "nice" places to work.

How would you describe your best high profile employees? The ones who really represent the essence of who you are and who you want to continue to become?

The people who do well here are the people who deal well with the many open-ended situations. They have good interpersonal skills. They figure out how to influence other people and participate in the whole process. They do this in some nontraditional ways sometimes.

For instance, one of our networking developers can be pretty tough. This individual has very strong opinions which can sometimes be devastating to others on the team. Even so, all of the people have learned to love him because he has good ideas and because he's determined to "come out and play ball." Once they get used to his particular style, they realize that he really is a good guy to work with. It's good that we have a variety of styles. We don't want too much homogeneity.

Do you have an orientation process for new employees?

Yes, we cover a lot of communication issues. We talk about some of the things that could get them into trouble. We talk about E-mail etiquette and the general sort of philosophy and doctrine of the way we do things around here. We're working on strengthening our orientation process. We spend a lot of time hiring people and making them interview with numerous people. The purpose of this process is covered in the orientation, but it needs to be more closely linked. Basically, people who come into WRQ have the expertise to do what is needed and to develop expanded roles.

We've always had this thing about hiring the absolute best. This is really important to us. As we have grown in the marketplace it has sometimes been hard to find the best people. Some people think, "We can *grow* technicians now—train them internally—since it's so hard to find people with the right technical characteristics. We have the infrastructure now and don't need quite the same level of autonomy and expertise anymore." Actually, this *isn't* true. We *do* need the same kinds of people. Every person we hire should be capable of more than what that position demands. We don't want people who have a self-imposed cap on their abilities. This is kind of a side doctrine of mine. If we're going to employ people who should be capable of doing anything, let's make sure we hire really bright people. We get a little lost in hiring people who meet specific technical characteristics. A lot of our best people have had oddball backgrounds.

Could you give us an example of this?

I remember back in 1986 when we got to the point that we needed to develop graphics display software. We wanted to hire some additional staff with background in this. We interviewed several people out of the high-tech industry from Oregon and also back at the North Carolina Research Triangle. It is humorous that the person we finally settled on would have seemed to *not* be the right person. We were looking for a person to do graphics on a PC in assembly language. The person we hired had never worked on a PC, didn't know assembly language, and had never done graphics.

This person was the best candidate because of a proven track record for being very smart, picking up new things, instantly accomplishing them, and continuously developing new projects. We would have been far worse off if we had hired any of the other candidates. Finding a technical person who has the ability to complete developing projects is the very best. The specific technical knowledge is not as important.

What you are describing is what many of the leading educators, particularly in secondary education, are trying to emphasize. It is the concept of learning to learn. We truly do not know how to prepare young kids.

Yes. Absolutely. That is true. I have a seven year old, and I have worked on some community programs where this comes up. I have served on a panel supporting the Resource Center for the Handicapped. We worked on getting handicapped people with recent injuries back into the workforce through computer usage. It is difficult to decide what curriculum is appropriate. Too often, people are interested in very specialized programs. We have a lot of industry people on these panels who say, "We do this in our industry so let's teach them this—and then they'll be good employees." This is narrow thinking. The students not only need to be taught specific technology, they need to be challenged as learners.

In hiring people you frequently find that if someone has been able to do something in depth in a technical area, or in any area, there is a transferability of skills. On the other hand, if people who are too much the generalist—know a little bit about a lot of things but haven't achieved real depth in any specific area—they haven't developed the discipline required to achieve deeper capabilities.

I am continually amazed at the crossover achievements of someone who is a specialist in an area such as sanskrit, for example. Even though I don't need sanskrit, I hire the person anyway because I believe the discipline required to learn sanskrit can be transferrable to other areas. I think this is important, and I've seen it work.

Another example is musicians. I am not a musician but becoming one is hard and requires discipline. A lot of musicians are good programmers.

Since your role has changed significantly over the years, do you have some key insights from these changes?

One of our problems is that we are not really business people. By this I mean we haven't come from a business background, and we were never managers prior to this. In other words, by some people's standards, we are a little bit unqualified for this job. We've been thinking about this a lot since we've been confronted with organizational growth issues. It is very stress-ful for the company and ourselves.

Anytime you grow, you have people who are used to doing things in small groups in a hands-on manner, and then sud-denly it's not a small group any more. This is a key issue. We ask ourselves, "What things do we let go of and what things do we try to be very directive about?"

A lot of managers think of themselves as team-oriented people, and they are. But they also have a lot of control and influence with the team. Maybe they are charismatic. Even if it's not formalized authority, they are very influential. The difficult tran-sition for them is when they have to let go of things. I mean, how much can they delegate? Some people are good delegators, and other people aren't. As partners, we used to keep a tight control and we don't anymore. There are now two levels be-tween the programmers and myself.

Until recently, McKibben and I were involved in managing engineering. We decided we had to get out of this hands-on activity and get a director of engineering. This transition was hard for everybody because people had felt a personal rela-tionship with us. They realized we were no longer up to the job but because of the personal ties, didn't want to let go either.

How did you handle this transition?

Basically, my approach to this particular problem was to go around and talk to the influential people in engineering. I let them know what the problem was. I told them McKibben and I would have to give up this aspect of our jobs. This open discussion got everyone to thinking. They realized things couldn't continue to work the same way and that we'd have to get a director of engineering. I like to let people know in advance that change is coming so they can be thinking about how we can solve transition problems.

So then we went to the next stage. We posed, then answered two questions, "What is the process that we will use to hire the vice president of engineering?" and "How will the people participate in it?" It was a nice long path so everyone had time to become mentally ready for the transition.

We asked them not to just think about it but to take ownership of getting this new person. I talk to people from other businesses who say, "I always get input from my people." I think to myself, "That's garbage." I'm glad you get some input but I don't want input. I want the people to *own* the process. I don't like that input idea. Input is okay but it's condescending. We asked various people in the development department to be on the selection committee and they actually had to hire the person.

Did you interview the candidates at some point before the final hiring decision was made?

Yes, I had authority in the process. In other words, I was on the final interview team. It would have been hard, at that point, to overrule the committee's selection. It would have sent the message, "I wanted you to own it but not really. Ha! Ha!" By encouraging participation, people raise the issues they think are important. This process actually worked pretty well.

Do you bring in outside resources to help with the firm's development, specific skill training or philosophical training, or does it mostly happen in-house?

A lot of what we do comes from in-house resources. We have also brought people in from the outside and have been open to doing more of that. I think it can be a good idea. Sometimes bringing in outside help has been disappointing. Recently we've been setting up stock option plans in our compensation area, and we found the national firms on compensation didn't deliver much help. It has been disappointing.

You just mentioned your efforts to provide stock option plans to your employees. Could you describe WRQ's reward system and how it works?

It's currently in flux, but there are some basic elements. Everybody has health benefits, a base salary, and a company-wide plan called the revenue bonus. This is based on company-established targets and a scale related to these targets. If we reach our targets, everyone gets 15% of their pay as a bonus. It's possible to scale as low as 0 and there is no upper limit. It has never been much below 15% but has been as high as 30%. The scale is determined using computable values.

Is the revenue bonus plan equally available to all employees?

Oh yes. Everybody is on the plan. There is also a discretionary bonus which is basically initiated by managers. People issue awards to others who are doing some sort of outstanding job. This is a less-defined compensation scheme, so it's impossible for me to give you a formula. All levels of people in the company are awarded these discretionary bonuses. It can be a very significant portion of their compensation, but it has a high standard deviation.

Could someone who is really entrepreneurial and has a great idea come to you or to one of the principals in your firm and suggest a new compensation method?

That could certainly happen. It's hard to imagine what that would be. We don't want to end up with a system that is totally arbitrary. Things are sometimes hard to compute so if you want a discretionary bonus system it needs to have some prime parameters and at the same time be sort of wide and loose.

I always contrast this idea with the school system. The nice thing about public school compensation is that it's entirely "fair." It is computable. You ask such questions as, "How much seniority have you got?" and "How many postgraduate course hours?" and with the answers to just a few questions, you can compute a person's salary.

Alternatively, you could do a little R & D and in a fairly short amount of time, with probably a certain error rate, get a pretty good idea of who the really good teachers are. But the problem with the educational model is that educators can't be rewarded for their exceptional teaching abilities because that would be arbitrary and quote, "unfair." So as an employer, you have to pick a scale that will actually have a degree of discretion when rewarding employees. The school system can't handle that, so they don't do it.

We have been writing our compensation philosophy. A lot of people suggest, "Our compensation can be perfectly fair." We say, "No. It is not necessarily fair." We like it to be fair but we also want to put an emphasis on giving rewards to people with a possible degree of arbitrariness—we do this so that we can recognize innovation and creativity. These are judgment calls and are difficult to compute.

Earlier you talked about WRQ's distributed authority system. Would you discuss how the system works to accomplish common business goals?

When you have a real distributed authority system, you still need something that ties things together. Otherwise people will ask: "Why don't we all just do fun things?" "What are we here for?" If you're going to have this kind of system, there needs to be a shared philosophy, and all the people need to work on it.

If you had been in the Chinese communist party years ago, you would have all shared in the "long march." That was the defining moment for the Chinese communist party. Their commonly shared philosophy was the primary thing that brought them together as a party. If an organization wants to have shared authority, there has to be a common philosophy. This is the key element.

Can you give an example of how the shared philosophy works at WRQ?

I'll give you an example using a simple process such as handling travel expense guidelines. Some organizations have a very thick book on how travel expenses are to be handled. They attempt to be fair. I suggest if a company has a travel *philosophy* that employees go by rather than following strict guidelines, people won't be inclined to do "anything they want." If there is some kind of shared philosophy, people can at least know an acceptable way of handling travel in the organization. You don't need a rule if you have a shared philosophy on travel expense. You do that instead of writing out the guidelines. That's the way we prefer to do it. We try to do that with all matters. When people get together to talk about these things, they want to write regulations. We don't want to write any more regulations. We always want to deal with issues philosophically.

I'm sure some employees have taken advantage of this process in the past but I believe that you'll get better buy-in and better adherence with a general philosophy than with extensive written guidelines. People can always figure a path through them. It becomes part of the game.

With a shared philosophy and a distributed authority system, do you use your own internal values as guidelines?

We are big on the respect system. Even though people will sometimes disappoint you, treating them with respect makes them more respectful. This philosophy of respect and trust is important when you have people working from home or from remote sites. Many employees do that here. There's no one at their homes to make sure they are following any guidelines. We believe, "If it works for the individual and for the company and something can be worked out, then it's probably okay." If you write regulations as if they were entitlements for a person to work at home and it doesn't work out well for the team—then it doesn't work. It's time consuming to write these regulations. You could make a career of it.

The question of renewing and sustaining self seems to come up more for empowering leaders who are highly interactive and choose to work in a collegial way. Have you thought about how you renew yourself and how that might spill over to others who work in this organization?

From an organizational perspective we talk about people taking a long-term view. We have been fortunate that the founders and all of the original partners, even those who have left, have wanted to see the organization sustained. We keep encouraging people to take the long-term view because it is important to the organization.

On a personal level, we tell everybody to keep a balance with their families. We emphasize personal life as part of a long-term view. Everybody works hard during crunch times, but if you work so much that you end up with your spouse wanting to divorce you, then that would be very distracting. There are organizational leaders who still believe that when an individual burns out, there is another one standing by the door to take his or her place. We make a long-term investment in people. Again, that is why we can hire somebody who doesn't meet specific technical requirements but who is a really smart person. There may even be a start-up cost, but we believe the long-term potential payoff is better.

If others noticed that someone was really focused on a particular project and worked too many nights in a row, would they nudge the person to cut back?

We emphasize this but we don't do it perfectly. In fact there are stories we tell about these kinds of situations. It is especially bad for managers to get strung out working too many hours.

I'm not a fan of the fellow but I once read a story written by General Patton that I thought was very good. He talked about the problem of burnout among the division commanders. Most of them were about 30 years old. They had been given command of 15,000 men and many of these men were dying in battle. It was a pretty serious situation. They didn't go home at night. They tended to work all the time and the cost was enormous. Patton talked about having a tired division commander who just "pulled an all nighter" and the effect this had on the 15,000 men. They were all tired the next day because the division commander was tired.

This is clearly transferrable to an organization like ours. There is always something pretty exciting to work on. So we nudge one another to keep the balance. It's too expensive *not* to. We don't want to lose division commanders or divisions because they have burned themselves out.

Do you tell stories, then, within your own company?

Oh, yes, we are definitely storytellers around here. Since none of us have formalized business school backgrounds, we do *not* use a lot of theory. We *do* know stories provide information and that *our* stories communicate our history, philosophy, and vision to each other. I've always liked stories. Lincoln was a great storyteller. We encourage others within our organization to share stories.

CHAPTER 10

GEORGE WALKER
REGIONAL VICE PRESIDENT
(RECENTLY RETIRED, US WEST COMMUNICATIONS)
SEATTLE, WASHINGTON

George Walker grew up in Seattle, attended public schools, and graduated from Queen Anne High School. He began working for Pacific Telephone on his eighteenth birthday. After the war he returned to the University of Washington to complete a degree in journalism in 1951. He is married, with two grown children.

Over the last forty-five years, Mr. Walker has participated in numerous organizational changes, including his first positions with Pacific Telephone, Pacific Telegraph and Telephone, American Telephone and Telegraph (AT&T), and Pacific Northwest Bell, where he was state vice president—chief executive officer for

Washington from 1983-1993. Walker recently retired as regional vice president for public policy for US WEST Communications with responsibility for the states of Washington, Oregon, and Utah.

Over the course of his forty-five-year career, Mr. Walker has served as a director, chairman, or board member of over twenty-two community organizations, among those director and past chairman of the Metropolitan YMCA Board; past chairman of the Economic Development Council of Seattle and King County; director of United Way of King County; director and past chairman of the board for the Fred Hutchinson Cancer Research Foundation; director of the Seattle Alliance for Education; director and past chairman of the board for Greater Seattle Chamber of Commerce; advisory board member of the Resource Center for the Handicapped; director of the University of Washington Foundation; the past chairman of the board and member of the executive committee and director of Leadership Tomorrow.

You have been in the telephone industry for a long time. Would you give us some background of this dynamic, changing industry?

When I began my career, the telephone company utilized electro-mechanical technology. Entry-level telephone operators were individuals who worked in huge buildings full of clicking switches and whose job duties included answering, "Hello, Central, This is Ethel." Today, telephone communication occurs through a solid state transistorized technology. The whole art of how communication has occurred in this country has meant changing how people did their jobs, and this included telephone operators, service representatives, the business staff, engineers, and members of the management and administrative team. Because of this, the telephone company has recently undergone "one of the most massive retraining jobs ever undertaken, before or since, in the history of the world."

The need for schools and businesses to work together in retraining has often been discussed. What does US WEST believe about school-business relationships?

Supporting education reform has been a corporate priority for US WEST. We want to improve the product that is coming out of the schools. Our traditional, basic, entry-level job was a telephone operator. Today, since so much is automated, this job has changed to directory assistance operator. We have found that 75 percent of the high school graduates who apply to be an assistance operator can't pass the entrance examination. They can't do even simple things such as alphabetizing. This is needed in order to use the automated equipment to find a telephone number. There are lots of good ideas regarding education reform and many of those have been discussed in the Washington Roundtable.

There have been a lot of mergers and reorganizations in the communications industry. How has this affected the work at US WEST?

We are in the midst of another major change now. Since I returned to Pacific Northwest Bell, there has been a total re-engineering process. The challenge we had in the last ten years was merging separate companies, including Northwestern Bell in the Great Plains states, Mountain Bell, and Pacific Northwest Bell. We have had to integrate three totally separate cultures and three totally separate business systems serving fourteen states.

The goal was to get the corporate cultures working together as opposed to working against each other. People needed to learn to work together internally in order to compete externally. It has probably taken ten years to combine the separate companies and cultures and there is still work to do to establish trust within the merged organizations.

What have been the most difficult parts of this change process?

The change in philosophy and structure has been difficult for some individuals. There have been some "dead bodies" as a result of this. There have been some people at every level of the business who couldn't adjust to the new working environment, and they are no longer there. The number of people has also been reduced through attrition and early retirement. Even so, we still have a long way to go.

Today we have very elaborate computer systems that have been brought into these companies over the last twenty-five years and these systems have led us into new technology delivery. Both the individuals and the systems have been driven about as fast as they can go. We have the problem of setting up new systems while keeping old systems going. Our situation is similar to trying to repair a moving train. We are beginning to re-engineer how we deliver service. It's almost as if we're starting with a blank sheet of paper. During this change we are looking at *what* everybody's job is, *how* they do their job, *where* they work, and *what* they use to do their job.

Over the years, have there been any specific events that have served as turning points as US WEST changed?

For me, it has been more of a continuing sequence of events. It has been the challenge of trial and error in working with others to adapt the business and work systems to the changing technology. The key issue for many employees is how to adapt to continual change. A few years ago when people were hired, there was a social contract that was understood between the employee and the employer. People had the potential for a long-term career, and unless they made great errors, they would continue with the company until they got sick or retired. If you use the metaphor of the moving train many traditional employees are now finding the train going in a different direction from what they expected, or it's going too fast and they are uncomfortable, so they have gotten off. The people whom we hire today have a different motivation.

In order to accomplish changes, we have had a number of meetings and seminars at different levels of the business. The first question we asked was: "Who is the customer and how do we deliver a quality service to that customer?" Our focus has been to move away from a traditional militaristic organization and to build the organization around this customer-focused process. This focus is based on our knowledge of what is happening at the customer level. The result has been to reduce levels in the organization and to use more of a matrix form of management.

What kind of impact has the new customer-service focus had on the organization?

There is a frequent problem that occurs in any organizational system, both here and in other companies. After the classroom training, the new managers receive their certificates proving that they've been taught to do certain things, and they get their telephone and their office. However, there is little follow-up on their learning. We need to know if that person is doing what they are supposedly trained to do once they are back on the job for about a month. We are constantly trying to improve on the feedback.

To illustrate, if you were to consider our traditional work organization, say ten years ago, we had a supervisor and a business office service representative to take orders for new business. The service rep would talk to you about your bill and take your order. Ten years ago we had six reps and six supervisors for every office. Service reps would ask supervisors about questions they couldn't handle. Now we have broadened the span of control. The supervisor may have twenty or twenty-one people instead of six. When this occurs you are going to have to work on a different basis, both from a training standpoint and from an empowerment standpoint. You need to be sure you have a system in place that enables the supervisor to supervise and the people to do their jobs well.

This is not just an organizational change which has been tried and has failed. You need to make sure when you change the system that you empower the individuals to be able to participate in a different way. Some of it is training, some of it is bringing people together with different ideas, and some of it is empowerment. We need to give employees the ability to delegate and to take risks.

Could you explain more of the whole concept of empowerment as the center of the current re-engineering of service centers at US WEST?

The re-engineering we are doing is creating mega centers for delivery of service. This is the opposite of what I described earlier, which is a traditional system of going through six different work groups. In that system, if the new phone service didn't work two days after installation, you started all over with somebody coming out to the house to fix the problem. A lot of duplication of service occurred by the time that process was completed.

That is the way it has worked until now. With the aid of technology we are in the process of creating the mega center to allow one person to have the necessary information to do everything. But it's not easy. When this procedure is in place, for example, if you move into a new home, by pushing a few buttons you'll be ready to use your telephone service. It won't happen all at once because the technology is expensive. We'll start in the urban areas where the demand can support the cost of the transition. That is the change we are in the midst of now and it requires a tremendous amount of energy. It's a new job altogether as opposed to a job anyone has ever done before. Some people will be able to supervise the job and some will not. Some will leave and some new employees will be hired. We're advertising the new job within the company, and some people are going to relocate in order to do it. This impacts communities. For example, Spokane now has about 850 employees and after many relocate, it will probably have about four hundred employees.

In an area that's even broader than cross-functional training, we'll be merging about twenty different business systems and many computer systems. We're also setting aside some of our traditional computer systems and building new ones. This is an example of what we are doing now in terms of cutting down the product cycle. This is typical of the challenges of many businesses.

How have you been able to sustain this organizational change over time?

You have to feel that you have the trust and support of others in making a change. Everybody in business works for somebody. If the person is the CEO, then that means he needs to be supported by the board of directors, and they need to be committed to what the CEO is doing.

We have a state board with good people on it. One of the mistakes CEOs in some organizations have made in the past is in the selection of board members. For example, they say something like, "I'll put you on my board and you put me on your board, and we'll both pay each other $35,000 per year in director's fees." Those kinds of boards have ended up with "good old boys"—members who were half retired or fully retired. When they retire they're on a dozen different boards and play golf together when they meet. You can't really get much substance out of a board structured that way.

You can really get in a tough position with acquisitions and hostile takeovers when you don't have a quality board. If each individual who is selected for the board is not bringing something to it, you're going to have problems. Dick McCormick is our chairman and CEO now, and I've worked with him on a couple of board appointments. He has some definite criteria he is looking for in candidates. Each will bring something different to the board to help make it more accountable.

As a company we have made some mistakes. One of the things we do to correct them is to discuss with board directors some of the directions we have taken. We have evaluated some of the mistakes and have worked to understand how they occurred. As a CEO, you have to be willing to say, "We have gone into this area or that area and it has cost us a lot of money." It is a courageous decision on the part of the CEO to say, "We were wrong, but we're going to move ahead." It requires open communication between the board and the CEO.

Mistakes are a form of learning. I have encouraged discussion of them during the last ten years. We've done a lot of things that are good and are on the leading edge. The most recent example has been the acquisition of 25 percent of an entertainment provider. We got in at a very good price and were the first company to move into that area. On the negative side, we've gotten into the real estate business heavily in the past and we lost money there. We realized after a while that we had no business being involved in that area. It ended up costing our stockholders some money to get out of it. We also got into the financial services business, and although we didn't lose a lot of money in that venture, we found that it detracted from other things we were doing. It took us a while to learn that we were better off when we stayed with our mission and our core objective and strength—connecting people—and not getting off into these other areas. Other companies have also learned this same lesson. About ten years ago we all thought about diversification, but we found our investors didn't want a diversified investment. None of us is perfect. When we make a decision, it is based on our awareness at the time.

Within this changing environment you have just described, how are employees at various levels rewarded for their contributions?

For most of the basic occupations, the reward system is based on the financial and service performance of the company. We have some very exacting standards for delivering service. They come to about 50 percent of an individual, or work group's, remuneration. We have financial objectives as well. As you can imagine, it depends upon your level in the company as to how much of your compensation is based on the performance of the company. In my case, over one-third of my compensation depended upon the service and performance of US WEST. So whether you like it or not, this structure forces you to put your heart into making the whole company successful, not just one particular department or one particular project. That tends to be a real motivator.

On the craft level, it becomes a moment of truth when you work with the unions. There you have the authority of organized labor influencing the nature of the commitment the employees are making. The result is that everybody keeps close track of the service performance when it makes a difference in terms of how much money will be paid.

The other thing we've done is provide stock options way down into our business, not just at the executive level. The second and third levels of management receive stock options. For a while the stock stayed even, and to a lot of people the stock option just looked like a worthless piece of paper. In the last several years, US WEST stock has gone up 22 percent. The price of stock went up from the high $30s to close to $50 per share earlier this year. So now, exercising the stock option has become attractive for many employees.

What are the effects of the organizational changes in relation to the new role the employees will be playing through the mega centers?

A lot of employees have taken early retirement. Some have made termination arrangements, and some will be laid off. It's the same for many businesses now. Individuals have so much data at their fingertips that not as many middle managers are needed. Now many employees benefit from the availability of spreadsheets and have an understanding of how to use them within their group. It's hard to believe so much change has occurred within the last ten years.

Forty-five years ago when I began, I worked in our company mail room. We had a room full of women (only women) and some of those rows of desks seemed to be a block long. People were sitting at their typewriters typing individual telephone bills. We all used a comptometer to calculate what the telephone charges were. The operator filled out little pieces of paper listing who you called, how long you talked, etc., and people typed up the bills one by one. You wonder how it ever worked at all.

What are the high-priority workforce issues you are facing today?

I think the one area we have done a lot of work in is developing awareness of diversity in the workforce. I believe that US WEST has done more work in this area for a longer period of time than most companies in the Northwest and probably any company nationally. Developing a diverse workforce is important from a societal standpoint, as well as being good from a business standpoint. All of our employees should reflect the makeup of the population of the United States. If you are going to be responsive to the customer body, you need to make sure you have people designing your products who can relate to and understand the diverse needs in society. It is the right thing to do socially, and it is also good business to have a diverse workforce.

In an effort to develop our workforce, we have each employee attend a three-day class at headquarters on issues of diversity. Before class each employee has a one-day on-site session. We have had every response you can possibly imagine to the training. Some have been very enthusiastic, others have gotten up and tried to leave, others have sat in class and read their newspaper, saying, "You can make us attend this class, but you can't make us listen or change." If you have a guy who normally works on a telephone pole in Montana, and you're telling him that he needs to learn more about the needs of gays and lesbians, you sometimes have a problem in terms of cooperation and participation. We say, "You either participate or you don't get paid."

Given your recent experience with major organizational change efforts, how have you been able to renew and sustain yourself?

The biggest mistake you see leaders and top managers make is that they rely on past successes. At some time in their career they may have done something that was very successful or created a business procedure or method that lifted them out of the masses. But if you follow their career and watch them, too many of them keep doing that same thing over and over again. The most effective leaders support innovation by letting others make some decisions, evaluate what they have done, and continue the cycle as the technology or the individuals change.

I have been able to sustain my own participation because I thrive on crisis and chaos. I get bored rather easily when the protocols are established and procedures are worked out and everything is going along well. Fortunately, we have enough change around here that it is really interesting. At this point in my life, I don't need to work, and I would not have continued to work if I hadn't enjoyed what I was doing. With some of the challenges we've just discussed, I have had an opportunity to participate in something of an innovative nature and pass that challenge on to others.

CHAPTER 11

BETTY WOODS
PRESIDENT AND CHIEF EXECUTIVE OFFICER
BLUE CROSS OF WASHINGTON AND ALASKA
SEATTLE, WASHINGTON

Betty Woods was born in Radford, Virginia, and attended public schools there. Woods holds a bachelor of arts degree in psychology from Seattle University and also has completed programs of graduate study at Stanford University and the Wharton School of the University of Pennsylvania. Woods also attended the National Health Care Institute at the University of Michigan. She is the mother of three children and has recently remarried. Betty Woods chose to stay home with her three children for ten years before she resumed her career.

Woods worked for a short time as a consultant before joining Blue Cross in 1976 as director of training and development.

Prior to her current position, she served as executive vice president and chief operating officer with responsibility for all operating functions.

Woods is currently the president and chief executive officer (CEO) of Blue Cross of Washington and Alaska, an organization of 1,200 and one of the largest health care contractors in the states of Washington and Alaska. Woods assumed the position of CEO in March 1993 and is the first woman in the nation to lead a Blue Cross Blue Shield organization.

Currently Woods serves on the Board of Trustees of the Greater Seattle Chamber of Commerce. She also serves on the Board of Directors for Beckman Instruments and Pacific NW Bank, and during 1994-1995 she served as vice chair of the Snohomish County Economic Development Council.

It is unusual for a training and development professional to become CEO of such a large organization. Tell us about your original career goals and development at Blue Cross.

People often ask me, "Did you plan to be CEO?" The reality is my move to Blue Cross just kind of happened. My kids were teenagers when I started contemplating the move to Blue Cross. My daughters were sixteen and fifteen, and my son was eleven. I was a college graduate and was working toward an MBA, working part-time as a consultant, and I was truly not available to my kids. I would be gone for periods of time, and then I would be home for a while. This was a lifestyle I wanted to change. I needed to be more available.

Working for Blue Cross was attractive because it was located only two miles from my home. I could work for Blue Cross and still go to my kids' school conferences, get them to their sports activities, and be there for them.

Another thing that made Blue Cross an attractive place to work was that it was growing rapidly, and the whole area of staff development and training was just beginning to be promoted inside the company. Until this time, the organization had offered no management or supervisory training. When I came in I was overqualified for the job, but I was willing to take a step backward in order to meet my personal needs. It proved to be a good move.

I was also becoming less comfortable in the consulting world. This was true for a couple of reasons. I was not comfortable with marketing myself and my abilities. I did not do it well and I felt my work should be able to speak for itself. Consultants who come to work for me today often rue the day I was a consultant because when they start marketing, I say, "Stop." The second reason I didn't like consulting, although I love organizational development, was that I was never really around an organization long enough to see how my efforts worked out in the long term. I decided I wanted to fully implement the theories of organizational development within my own work environment. I wanted to see my efforts through the long term.

Anyway, I came to Blue Cross and my department immediately grew from one person to about six because there were trainers in various parts of the company, and it was felt they should be working together out of one place.

Were you an empowering manager back then? How did you work with your staff to empower them to get the work accomplished?

I didn't use the word empowerment back then. I believe in holding people accountable for the job they have been asked to do. In the early years I learned an incredible amount about how people try to get rid of accountability. They will try to give it back to you and they'll try to give it to others. But through the years I've learned how to hold people accountable.

I have established a reputation in this company. People know if I ask them to do something, then I'm going to hold them to it. They also know if I tell someone I will do something, that person can trust that I'll do it. So there's a trust that has to be developed over time. I also strongly believe when you hold people accountable that you can't ask them to do something they're not trained to do, that they don't have resources to do, or they don't have the environment in which to do it. So, in order to hold people accountable, which is the foundation of empowerment, you have to create an environment in which people *can* do what you have asked them to do. The key question then becomes: "How do you do that?"

One way to do this is to create that environment. After being here eighteen years, I can tell you this is easier said than done. You just keep chipping away at it. You also have to hold people who work for *you* accountable for holding the people who work for *them* accountable. Accountability cascades down. There also must be consequences. When I started with Blue Cross there were no consequences for not doing a good job. Likewise, if you did do a good job, the consequences were that you got more work. I am an example of this.

People need to have clarity about what is expected of them. Over the years, all the people who have worked with me have had performance appraisals like they've never had before. In any event, there were no surprises. It is one of the most effective things I have learned. Now most of the people who work for me do appraisals the same way. We ask the people who report to us to answer a few questions before we give them their performance appraisal. These questions include "What have you accomplished according to your plan? What have you done that you didn't plan to do, and what did you plan to do that you didn't do? And why?" Basically, they are giving themselves a performance appraisal. When you force them into answering these questions, you force them into planning. The process is behaviorally-based, and it is realistic.

As I took on more organizational responsibility, I held to this philosophy. One of my largest frustrations was to have peers who didn't do any of this. They said they'd not have time because they were, first of all, technicians. One of the strengths I bring to this job and to the job I had as chief operating officer is that I'm a generalist. I am not an accountant, an actuary, or a data processing person. I consider my profession to be management, and I have always considered it that.

It was frustrating for me to have peers who didn't hold their employees accountable. This caused organizational inequities. I had to live with other company employees who were paid more than my staff or who were rewarded unfairly because they were not being held accountable. That was difficult.

Do you have examples which demonstrate some of your management challenges prior to becoming CEO?

One of the major stories that really reinforced my management philosophy was in 1989 when I became chief operating officer (COO). We were in severe financial trouble at that time. We had seven days of reserves, and we had hit the bottom of the underwriting cycle. We were in tremendous trouble financially. We didn't know if we were going to survive. So, we put together a recovery plan.

It was one of the worst times in my career, but it was also one in which I learned a lot. I lived and breathed my job. I basically was so stressed when we finally reached a plateau that I said I needed to take some time off. I took a two-month sabbatical. People said, "Why are you taking time off at this point in time?" My answer was, "So I can stay!"

In addition to doing all of the survival activities, we had a workforce of about two thousand employees. They were scared to death because they knew that we might have to do more downsizing. We had already laid off over three hundred people. The trust was gone. This high-stress work situation went on for about two-years from '88-'89.

It was a bureaucratic organization and by this time I had a feeling of where the problems were. I thought they were at the mid-manager level. In late 1989 we conducted one of our Employee Opinion Surveys. We do these every other year. In the past, I had put the surveys together and then had them administered. I counted on my peers to work with their own areas of responsibility.

Now I was in charge as COO. When I got the results back, I used the consultant who had helped us build the survey. I told my staff, "I'm going out and I'm going to talk to every employee." It was like I threw a grenade into the various departments.

Management responded with, "You can't do that." So I said, "Fine, they are my employees and not only am I going to talk to them, I'm going to talk to them without you being there." The consultant then came in and said, "You can't do that. You have to allow the vice presidents and managers to stay in charge and as involved as possible." I wondered—if there was nothing to worry about, why was everyone so concerned about me talking to their employees?

It was a wild time. I had the survey results split out according to department which also included supervisory areas with twenty or more employees. This was done in order to maintain anonymity for the employees. Because of all the concern, I adapted my original plan and told them, "I'll do it this way. I will have you (vice presidents) look at your survey results, and you tell me what you think your issues are *before* I talk to your people. Then I'll still talk to the employees, and then I'll come back and talk with you. Together we'll decide what the issues are, and I promise you that nobody will be fired the first year."

None of them had ever had a manager talk directly to their staff or communicate with them. In my opinion, next to accountability, communication is the next fundamental foundation for empowerment. This is where it got hard, and it took an inordinate amount of my time to complete this process. My background was in organizational development and this was a major effort.

I learned so much about my officers during this time. When referring to the survey comments they would ask, "What about this and this? Where are they saying this, this, and this?" I talked to employees by department, by area and by vice presidential area. This was all about integrity.

I met with the employees in groups of fifty to seventy. The managers were not there, and I even had employees ask me if their assistant supervisors could be excluded. Nobody had ever done this kind of intervention before. I closed the door and I said, "Here are the corporate results and here are the results of your area. I'm not here to tell you what the issues are but to ask *you* what they are." It was an incredible process!

They said they had been waiting for somebody to ask them what they thought. They told me all about their concerns. They told me about their management. I went back to their production areas. I witnessed the working conditions in some of those areas, and—I was embarrassed. There were times when, if a particular vice president had walked down the hall, I probably would have done what I'd promised I wouldn't do—which is fire the person on the spot. But, I had promised them I would not, so I didn't.

There were times when it was so overwhelming to learn about a particular work environment it made me kind of sick. I hate to say that about my company, but it's not the same any more. We have a different company today.

After that I started the pressure for change with the middle managers because that was where the survey data and focus groups focused. I sat down with each vice president and said, "Here are the issues in your area, pick the top three for your performance appraisal for the next year. *You* determine how *you* are going to turn this around. People are as important as the financial goals of this organization. You have to follow this process with your managers as well." I have never been so autocratic!

The other thing I found was that about one third of our employees didn't know who their managers were and had never even seen him or her. I then stipulated that managers meet with their employees every month as part of their own personal performance plan. In addition to this, I let them know I would be going back to the employees in the coming year. I told them I was going to again conduct focus groups and ask the employees, "What has changed, and how has it changed?"

Then, I had to discuss boundaries with the employees. It took about three focus groups for them to get it. I asked them, "What is your role and what is your accountability in this company?" The first few times I asked that question, they answered, "We don't have any." I said, "Oh yeah, you do. Here is what they are."

How did you help your staff learn to handle the difficulties of taking responsibility for their actions and becoming more accountable?

If you have a problem with your boss, you are now accountable to tell him or her before you report it to anyone else. The boss *has* to have the opportunity to solve the problem and it can't be solved if the boss doesn't know there's even a problem. At first employees responded that they were afraid of retribution. I let them know they should talk to me if that happened. I told them they had a responsibility to first risk giving their boss feedback. If they didn't do this first, they had no right to complain to their co-workers because they were giving them information that their boss hadn't been given. You know, this worked.

Over the next year I began working with the departments that had the worst problems. I met with thirty employees every month. The employees learned they could rely on me to do what I had promised I'd do, and the managers knew I was keeping tabs on them. The vice presidents and managers were really upset with me because they felt I had gone around them. They would say, "You have usurped me, Betty." I would answer, "I have to find out what you need so I can help you do your job better. I need to know what kind of training you need and what kinds of things I can do to help you become a better manager." It actually turned out to be a positive thing for the managers because I *really* supported them in what they were trying to do.

I offered them a chance to grow and change but what was really happening was that I was changing the rules on them, and I knew that. I said, "You've never been asked to do what I'm asking you to do." When you change the rules, you also have to offer them a fair game. So I also told them I would be there to help them grow and to provide them with learning opportunities.

Was everyone able to make the necessary changes or did some choose not to make the change?

Some things happened which leave me very sad. We had one vice president who responded to the changes with "I am not that kind of manager. I am a production manager. My job is to get the numbers and I will not play this stupid game." The only response I could offer was, "Then you have to leave because these are the rules here." He did leave. That was his choice.

I also had a couple managers who were stars and on a fast track. What I found out was that they were doing it on the backs of their employees. They were taking their employees' ideas and making them their own. They were not treating their employees well. They were shocked when I found out. Two of those managers, whom I thought had tremendous potential, couldn't look themselves in the mirror. They were not secure enough to make that bridge, and they left as well. I was sad for them because they had an opportunity to grow and mature but chose not to take it.

How have you continued your communication efforts now that you have been in the CEO job for a while?

This story begins when I first took charge. I believe we have been a paternalistic organization and that we've treated our employees like children. What the organization ended up with was people coming to whine to you all the time. I stopped allowing people to do that. I said, "I'm going to treat you like adults. I expect you to act like adults. I will always tell you the truth so don't second-guess me. Don't politicize what I have told you because I'll always tell you the truth." My motto has been to do that. In the process employees are empowered.

I still have focus groups every couple of months. The focus groups are now done across the company. At the first of the year we send out a memo asking, "Do you want to talk to Betty? If you do, clip off the bottom of this coupon and send it in, and we will call you." The focus groups comprised people who want to talk with me.

We typically have about 30-35 employees in a group. The format is they can ask me about anything and I can ask them anything. I reserve some time for me. We also have our focus group communication in a newsletter that goes out to all employees. It's nothing fancy, just different colored paper containing the questions that were asked and my answers.

**In your current role as CEO, do you continue to take respon-
sibility for all communication or do you transfer responsibility for some organizational communication to others?**

One of the things I'm trying to do now is make the transition
to having people talk to other leaders in the organization as
well as to me. Being the kind of leader I am can create depen-
dencies. People say, "Why don't you talk to Betty?" We're getting ready to restructure and to do town meetings with all the
employees. That responsibility has been transferred to others.

I'm also conducting leadership training for all the managers.
One of the issues we get into is that some people don't want
to buy the whole idea of public accountability. They think
empowerment is doing anything they want. If they have a
hobby they like, they think that they should be able to do it. If
you tell them they can't then they think you're telling them
they're not empowered. We had this problem in 1990-1991, so
I developed three over-arching goals.

Empowerment means looking at a situation, answering every question connected to it, taking responsibility, and then—
if what you want to do meets the following criteria—go do it.
The first criterion is financial well-being, which is our number
one goal. The second is: Does it benefit the customer? The
customer is the centerpiece of this organization. Ask yourself:
Is what you want to do only for *your* convenience—to make
your life easier—or does it make the customer's life easier? If it
makes your life easier does it make the customer's life harder?
The third criterion is a bias for action in terms of being empowered: If it meets the other two criteria, know how you are
going to go about doing it.

When I became CEO in March, after being chief operating
officer for five years, the employees were so accustomed to
me being available to them that there were some very rough
times while we did some re-engineering. I guess I would be
described as the type of leader who can be tough. I can force
people, push them, drive them, and be rigid but supportive at

the same time. They were accustomed to that style. So when I became CEO I needed to do something to change the process of communication because there was a tendency for them to want me to stay internally focused. Earlier, as the COO, about 70 percent of my job was internally focused. As the CEO, about 70 percent of my job was externally focused. They haven't liked this change because I had become their security. I let them know a new chief operating officer would be taking over the internal responsibilities, and they needed to learn to work with this person the same way they had worked with me.

How did you prepare yourself for your new duties as CEO?

On March 1, I became CEO. Just before this, I took about two weeks off. I went to Montana for a week of skiing and then spent a week at a spa in Tucson. I just needed to go off by myself for renewal. Even then I worked about three hours a day developing an inaugural speech to my employees. When I came back, I had my former boss and a good friend who lives in Dallas read it. I value both of their opinions. They suggested a couple of changes, and on March 5th I called all the managers together. We did a satellite transmission from here to all the branch offices in Washington and Alaska. I spoke directly to all employees as their new CEO.

Now that you have instituted new ways of holding people accountable and have increased communication, how would you characterize the organizational health today?

Actually we now have 1,100 employees. We have downsized in the last three years. Even so, employees are happier. Many have been involved in the re-engineering efforts.

Another thing I learned from the focus group meetings was how bored many employees were with their jobs. Clerical jobs had been specialized to the "nth" degree. There was no variety. The re-engineering efforts allowed us to put employees in new situations. The production areas were organized into teams including cross-functional teams, and we have now been doing this for two years. They are excited, and the employees who are involved in this are happy. Even allowing for the economy and downsizing, our turnover has gone from about 15 percent to 7 percent. Employees don't want to leave.

When I gave the inaugural speech, I simply said to them, "I give my employees my heart, and my mind." As I completed the speech, I said, "Anything you need to know about my regime as CEO is right here in this speech." It was fascinating. The managers again said, "That is really great!" We made copies for them. They made copies for their employees and soon every employee had a copy.

Then two months later the place started getting chaotic because health care reform was implemented. My management staff started reverting back to some of their old behavior. So I called a meeting with all of them, including the supervisors. They were very shocked about my concerns until they had time to think about them. I told them I was disappointed and suggested that they were either part of the problem or part of the solution, but right now everybody in the room was part of the problem. I pointed out that we were not listening to the organizational values. "What values?" they asked. I knew they were going to ask this. I pointed at our values statement and said, "Right here!" "Oh, *those* values!" they said. I just keep putting the values statement back to them.

It is difficult because we are again going through some incredibly difficult times as an industry and as a company. We have to downsize again. We have put a strategic plan together which is very aggressive. We're totally restructuring the company because we can't get to where we need to be with the current structure. It's a matter of survival. I was out of town after the board approved the strategic plan. In my absence my direct reports, who were members of the corporate council, called a meeting of all employees and shared the approved plan with them.

How did the employees respond to the meeting?

The only place we could find that was big enough was a historical building built in 1910 with an auditorium that holds about 1200 people. We bussed people over there for the two-hour meeting in the afternoon. We then did a second meeting, and I was there this time. It was important for me to be there and to show them how much reduction we were going to have. I showed them the numbers. I told them why the numbers were this way, and I told them I didn't have all the answers but I said, "Remember what I told you before: As soon as *I* know more, *you* will know more." It was a very successful meeting.

Basically I ended the meeting by saying, "I can't always be the one to talk to you, but whoever is standing up here is my spokesperson. They are here with my information, so listen. We are going through tough times. I know you're all scared. Sometimes we all have to live with ambiguity for a time. That is a requirement. I can't guarantee you employment but what I can promise you is employability if you stay with me because you are going to have to learn additional skills. You are going to have to stretch more than you've ever stretched before."

I firmly believe, in terms of communication, that people don't always get it the first time. They often have to hear it at least three times, especially when it is a tough message. You have to keep telling them, and it has to be consistent.

We also instituted town meetings because I knew the employees were going to continue to have a lot of questions. Attendance was not mandatory. The meetings were held at lunch time, so attendance was on their own time. They were invited to bring their lunches and to ask any questions that they had. We had a lot of employees attend.

Before the second meeting, I talked with the managers ahead of time because a lot of them were going to be affected and because I thought the message was so critical. I started with the vice presidents. I said, "I want you to sit through this *every time* I deliver it. You need to understand it and be able to explain it to employees." I then had meetings with the managers and then with the supervisors. Each time the prior groups joined the next groups. After hearing the message a few times several of them commented, "You're right. Every time I hear it, it makes more sense."

I also didn't want the officers to be sitting in the same room with the managers when they heard it for the first time. Everybody always asks, "What does this mean to me?" The officers needed to be able to ask questions without having the managers who reported to them present in the same meeting.

Employees need to feel secure, and I don't mean secure in terms of job security because I don't think there *is* any today. They need to feel secure in their leadership—that it is approachable, consistent, and credible. When this happens, they feel empowered. I take empowerment to be the employees' ability to come and tell you what they think. They should be able to go to their boss and say, "I don't like what you just did, or I don't agree with what you just did, or I don't agree with this solution, but let's find another way to do it." I think that is empowerment.

As COO and CEO, what has been, and is, your relationship to the board of directors during various organizational changes?

At the point in time I was COO, I didn't report to the board. I reported to the CEO. He trusted me when I came to him and said, "Here is what I'm going to do." He suggested I should be letting my managers do certain things. I told him I felt they were part of the problem at that time and asked him to trust me.

He supported me 100 percent. When I came back to him and reported what I had found, he was very surprised. He then said, "What are you going to do about it?" He was an empowering leader and he also knew I was making this organization mine since he had told the board he would be leaving in the next two years and I was to be his successor.

These major organizational changes take a lot of time and energy. How do you sustain yourself over the long term?

Well, after getting through a divorce about ten years ago, work has been sustaining. I also have a very strong spiritual side. I feel I need to know myself. I spend some time in counseling—from time to time to keep my head clear.

We all gather experience from the past and we carry it with us and it affects the way we behave. I, very intentionally, try to keep myself as clear as I possibly can. I go in and out of counseling, and I choose counselors who help me...by sort of being my confidante. About 95 percent of the time the counseling is to help me deal with work issues.

I have also learned over the years not to get too depleted. When I took that two month sabbatical back in 1989, I was about as depleted as I had ever been. I had suffered a personal tragedy several years before, and it was affecting other relationships. All that had been building up, and my approach in a crisis was to go to work. Some people drink. Some people eat. Some people do whatever—I work because I can get lost in it.

I said I'd never let myself become that tired again because I now give so much of myself that if I don't get something back, everybody pays. I have to keep finding ways to get something back.

During my sabbatical I went to Stanford for two weeks for an executive development program in marketing. What I have done since is to go to a spa once a year. Friends offer to go with me but I keep that as my personal time since I have so much other interaction in my life. I need to go alone.

I have a number of friends and some key friends who understand me. We've gone through a lot together. Through the years, I've had to let go of relationships that were not beneficial to me. They were beneficial to the other person, but they were not beneficial to me. I have a harder time letting go of women friends than men friends because I feel an obligation there. I am very intentional about myself now.

I have an acupuncturist. I am in the health care field, and I go to an acupuncturist! I also exercise. One of the problems I'm having right now is that my schedule is such that I haven't had the time to exercise and I'm beginning to feel it. Sometimes I take a day off or take a weekend and go to Methow and ski. That, considering the kind of leader that I am, is a part of being an effective leader. I think women do a better job of taking care of themselves than men.

You have really provided a full picture of your career at Blue Cross. Is there anything else you would like to add?

There is one other thing I didn't talk about that I think is very important and that is why I am in this profession in the first place. My motivation is achievement. My motivation is to see if I can make a difference. The reward is that I get to see if what I am trying to do actually works. That doesn't mean compensation is not important to me. I have worked with many people over the years. I have found people in my position are strapped financially sometimes even though they are paid well. Because they are living on the edge financially, decisions they make about their company are sometimes influenced by their own financial situation. Years ago I made a decision that I was going to have enough income to tap at any point should I want to walk away. The world changes. There is no security. So if I want to walk, or if someone else wants me to walk, my financial situation is fine.

I choose to be here and I choose to live simply. I choose not be a part of the Hollywood side of being a CEO. I don't know how else to say it.

WAKE-UP CALL

It doesn't matter whether you are from Seattle or Baltimore, Tokyo or Paris; whether you work in civil service or retail, high-tech or banking; whether you are an educator or a learner, a scholar or an observer; whether you lead an organization or support its mission—these stories apply to you. They apply because they offer examples of continuous learning, success-ful empowerment strategies, and personal integrity—all of which are necessary if one is to survive and flourish in today's busi-ness economy.

As you have read these stories, you have learned that em-powerment is a complex issue. It is often just as difficult to *empower* as it is to be *empowered*. In today's changing work-place, employees want to participate in decision making, but they also seek guidance and direction. Leaders want to include workers' opinions, yet they must provide the organizational context and structure needed for such open dialogue. In this process leaders and workers alike must assume responsibility and accountability for defining new boundaries. Each must respect and trust the other.

The outstanding leaders interviewed in this book suggest that they are on a journey and do not have all the answers. Their democratically-run organizations are culturally diverse and profitable and their employees are productive. They adhere to personal core values which are closely aligned with organizational goals. Their stories are practical, honest, authentic, courageous and inspiring. Their experiences challenge us to embrace learning and share leadership—THE KEY IS TO BEGIN.

How To Contact the Authors and Publisher

For public speaking, workshops or consulting in the areas of human resources, leadership and/or organizational development contact:

Kristine Sullivan Ed.D.
P. O. Box 1538
Mercer Island, WA 98040
206/232-6420 Voice Mail Messaging

For business trade publication proposals and manuscript submissions contact:

Johnna L. Howell
President
Integrity Publishing
7456 E. Greenlake Drive N.
Seattle, WA 98115
206/524-5348 • 206/524-5527 FAX
johnnahowl@aol.com

Also by **Integrity Publishing**

BOOK

Tools for Facilitating Team Meetings
by Johnna L. Howell
352 pgs, 8 X 11, ISBN 1-886671-00-1